Saunders-Roe

Anglesey Ltd

Builders of the world's lightest buses

Gerald Truran

First published in Great Britain in 2009
by Bryngold Books Ltd
Golden Oaks, 98 Brynau Wood, Cimla,
Neath, South Wales SA11 3YQ.
www.bryngoldbooks.com

Typesetting, layout, editing and design
by Bryngold Books

ISBN 978-1-905900-10-7

Printed and bound in Wales by
Gomer Press, Llandysul, Ceredigion.

Contents

Dedication

O n behalf of my late husband, I would like to dedicate his last book to all the former employees of Saunders-Roe. Without their efforts and achievements, Gerald's interest in the company would never have begun and the history of the company's buses would have remained unrecorded for future generations.

The book represents the collation of material from a 50 year interest in Saunders-Roe. Where possible, with the invaluable assistance of David Roberts and staff at publishers Bryngold Books, it remains true to the spirit of the original draft manuscript and thus reflects Gerald's enthusiasm in the company's history and its products.

Without the support of family and friends, the difficulties faced in realising such a project may never have been overcome. In particular, I would like to thank JG Nicol, P Platt, Colin Scott and Byron Westlake for their assistance in reading Gerald's manuscript along with M Fenton for allowing use of one of his photographs. In addition, I would like to express my appreciation to JG Nicol for contributing the foreword and allowing the photographs to be preserved for the future.

Finally, as a tribute to Gerald's memory, a donation from any proceeds from the sales of this book will be made to his favourite charity, The Royal National Lifeboat Institution. From the outset, Gerald wanted a charity working in Anglesey to benefit from the book's publication and as an island community he felt the RNLI was the perfect choice.

Margaret Truran
2009

Foreword

I first met Gerald Truran when he visited Beaumaris as a member of a council delegation to finalise the specification of refuse vehicles that they were about to purchase.

We soon identified a mutual interest in buses and spent some hours in my office during which time I was astounded by his depth of knowledge of the bus industry. I was therefore delighted to assist when, some months later, he proposed writing the history of bus production at Beaumaris. At his sad death I assumed the project had died with him, but was greatly pleased to learn that his family was determined to bring his work to fruition.

The factory at Beaumaris was located in a remote rural area of Britain, which was ideal for its purpose during World War II, but with poor links to the main centres of industry, not the best place during peacetime. To establish a successful bus building facility therefore, with the levels of production eventually achieved, was astounding.

I was employed at the factory all my working life and witnessed the output of a great variety of buses and lorries as well as marine craft and a bewildering array of other engineering products.

The site is still in existence but no longer a factory. The company was sold to the German licensor of the refuse vehicles being built there which was later based at a purpose built unit at the Anglesey county town of Llangefni.

During the lifespan of the works the name of the company changed several times due to amalgamations and takeovers, but to all the old hands who worked there and to many of the local community, it will always be known as Saunders-Roe.

I would like to look upon this book as a tribute to all those who worked at Beaumaris and also in memory of the man who aspired to write its history.

J G Nicol
Retired Engineering Director,
Laird (Anglesey) Limited.

Appreciation

T he contributions of many people have made this book possible. I would like to thank Mr JG Nicol, former quality control manager of Laird (Anglesey) Ltd and his colleagues at Beaumaris for their assistance. Despite various management changes over the years, Mr Nicol managed to retain a number of photographs, negatives and documents. Without his interest in the subject, I would have been unable to start my work.

I am also grateful for the individual contributions of J Bennett, J Cooper, R Davis, M Fenton, B Goulding, A Griffin, A Hall, R Kell, G Morant, R Phillips, P Platt, R Shaw and P Yeomans.

All the photographs in the book, except where shown, are reproduced from the Saunders Shipyard & Engineering Company Collection with the kind permission of Laird Group PLC.

The archive section of the British Commercial Vehicle Museum at Leyland provided much of the chassis information and I am very grateful for their help. The late I Owen of Saunders-Roe, D Jones (New Zealand) and Marshall Motor Bodies also provided information on the Beaumaris products. The New Zealand Omnibus Society contributed information on Saunders products supplied to New Zealand. The M&D East Kent Bus Club, Southdown Enthusiasts Club and the Crosville Enthusiasts Club were also most helpful.

Useful sources of information from the technical press included Bus & Coach, Passenger Transport, The Commercial Motor, Transport World, Buses Illustrated, The Saro Progress, the Saunders-Roe in-house journal; The AEC Gazette, The Aeroplane, Flight and the Leyland Journal.

The following books were also consulted: Liverpool Transport Volume IV, RT by K Blacker; Sowing the Seed by W Crossland-Taylor; Shorts Aircraft since 1900 by CH Barnes. An article on Beaumaris by David J Smith, published in the Aviation Magazine, provided information on the wartime activities at the factory. For a complete and detailed account of the Saunders business and the Saunders-Roe aircraft, Peter London's book, Saunders & Saro Aircraft since 1917 is invaluable.

Gerald Truran

The lightest buses

Throughout its long and distinguished history the name of Saunders Roe has been associated with innovation and development on land, sea, air and even in the exciting world of space technology. For a decade of its existence the company prided itself on a more down-to-earth operation — producing what it described as the world's lightest bus bodies.

These endeavours, in the years that followed the end of the Second World War, centred on the company's factory at Beaumaris, North Wales. Between 1946 and 1956 a total of 1,894 public service vehicle bodies left the factory, many for use in the United Kingdom, but many more for export worldwide.

The enterprise began in response to the need to satisfy three major demands of the immediate post-war years: to create jobs in an area of high unemployment, to produce goods for export and as a result help ease pressure on the Treasury to reduce the balance of payments.

More important perhaps was a dire shortage of new buses. At the end of the war, the nation's bus operators were forced to utilise vehicles which would normally have been long since retired. This created an urgent demand for the production of new replacement vehicles for the home market, but it would take time for the pre-war chassis and body manufacturers to realign their production from the war effort to satisfy the needs of peacetime bus companies.

This situation was worsened by the fact that in order to improve the balance of payments, manufacturers were encouraged to use any available supplies of raw materials to produce items for export. In addition to this, government departments chose to grant licenses for the purchase of raw materials only to companies manufacturing for export.

As a result, bus operators faced immense problems in their efforts to procure new vehicles. Even those who could afford to pay were denied them, while foreign companies struggling to pay for their orders were afforded a ready supply.

The harsh reality of this was that established bus manufacturers could never hope to satisfy the immense demand for new vehicles within the required time.

When they did consider producing new buses, the supply of bodywork remained the greatest issue. This problem enabled many companies not previously involved with the passenger transport industry to begin manufacturing or repairing bus bodywork. Saunders-Roe was one. They stood apart from others however, for unlike many new entrants into the industry, the company was not content to remain just another manufacturer. It was determined to become an innovative company and lead the way. This it did by introducing aluminium alloys for bodywork.

Many of the bodies supplied to customers, both at home and overseas, were produced in co-operation with notable chassis manufacturers such as AEC, Foden, Guy, and Leyland. The company created single and double deck designs, priding itself on providing durable, strong and lighter bodies that offered operators a long, trouble free operating life coupled with favourable economy.

This progressive thinking may however, have contributed to the company's eventual withdrawal from the bus industry. In the early 1950's, the cost of aluminium alloy used in the later products, coupled with the downturn in demand for new vehicles,

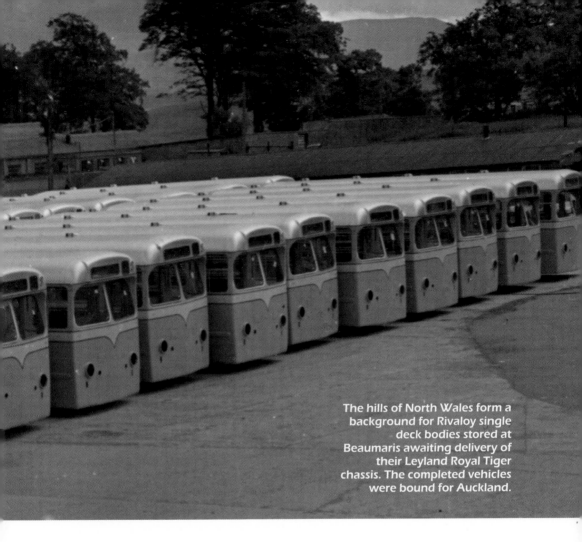

The hills of North Wales form a background for Rivaloy single deck bodies stored at Beaumaris awaiting delivery of their Leyland Royal Tiger chassis. The completed vehicles were bound for Auckland.

were both factors which heavily influenced the company's management. In addition, many of the ideas incorporated within the later designs failed to establish themselves until more than 20 years later, long after production ceased at the Beaumaris factory.

It is difficult to bring to mind another company which produced a bus body in quite the same form as the Saunders-Roe partially knocked down (PKD) body for the single deck chassis. In this respect, it was a true pioneer.

The use of jig assembly in its later body designs provided the company with the facilities for accurate production techniques though at considerable initial cost. Ironically, this expense was eventually justified through the realisation of large, single deck body orders for overseas operators. Amazingly, 67 per cent of the total body production at Beaumaris was exported and single deck bodies accounted for 80 per cent of total bodywork production during the period from 1946 to1956. In 1951 Saunders-Roe undertook the large-scale assembly of single deck bodies for a Cuban order and, as a result, was responsible for 70 per cent of all bus bodywork exported from the United Kingdom. This was a remarkable achievement for a company which

A side-frame unit is assembled on a double sided erection jig. Only bolting and riveting is required, panels, pillars and rails having been pre-drilled and brackets attached in the sub-assembly stage.

had started production of bus bodywork from scratch only five years earlier.

In 1950, following the general introduction of under-floor engined, single deck bus chassis, UK operators became concerned with the increased unladen weight of vehicles, causing a marked drop in fuel consumption figures. While pleased with the new and increased seating capacity, the difference in fuel consumption, between one and two miles per gallon, compared less favourably with the older, vertical front engined buses.

Companies within the large BET and Tilling Groups led the movement for lightweight single deck buses with a large seating capacity. This desire to reduce operating costs was understandable at a time of declining passenger numbers. As a result, buses of

Ten left hand drive Leyland Royal Tiger vehicles await shipment to Cuba.

lightweight construction appeared, sometimes featuring a spartan, external and internal appearance.

This however did not apply to the lightweight Saunders-Roe bodies. Made from aluminium alloy, they sported a notable design both inside and out meeting the need for a long operating life at minimal cost. The Saro single deck body was guaranteed to last 15 years at a time when most others had a design life of only 10. Unfortunately, the advantages of the Saunders-Roe body were not fully exploited, due to the accounting methods of many operators and changes in vehicle dimension regulations. It is hard to imagine just how such an innovative company would have prospered with the greater use of aluminium alloy in the bus body manufacturing process during the 1990s. Nevertheless, in or around 1953, the Saunders-Roe management decided to discontinue the production of bus bodywork at the Beaumaris factory. Instead, the business concentrated its efforts on work for government agencies and as a result, security measures were increased at the factory.

The last bus bodies to leave there were built in 1956 to fulfill an order from Auckland, New Zealand. This brought to a close an interesting period in the history of the Saunders-Roe company in particular and the transport manufacturing industry in general.

As a true testament to its innovate designs, many of the products of the Beaumaris factory remain in existence to this day. Although some are in the hands of vehicle preservation groups, others

Mounted on Daimler Freeline chassis, PKD bodies for New Zealand are packed ready for shipment. The front and rear ends are positioned on top of the left-hand chassis while the body sides are on the centre chassis. Already fitted, the roofs, small interior fittings, saloon floors and step plans are stored on the right-hand chassis.

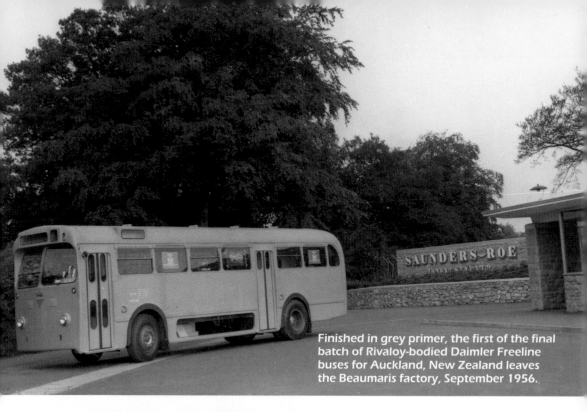

Finished in grey primer, the first of the final batch of Rivaloy-bodied Daimler Freeline buses for Auckland, New Zealand leaves the Beaumaris factory, September 1956.

remained in revenue earning service, as long as 40 years after leaving Anglesey.

Bus bodies only reflected one of the company's many interests however and after its sale the factory continued production of a variety of bodies for road vehicles for a number of years.

One of the Rivaloy-bodied Leyland Royal Tigers supplied to the Argentinian government.

Company origins

The origins of Saunders-Roe stretch back to 1830 when Moses Saunders set up a business in the village of Streatley, Berkshire, building locks and weirs on the River Thames. As it expanded it also diversified into boat building.

Following his death in 1859, the business continued to grow and additional factory space was acquired at Goring in 1870 and then South Stoke during the 1880s. Under the management of Sam Saunders the company experimented with the development of high-speed, powered boats and invented a new method of hull covering using laminated plywood. This was gradually improved and in 1898, the system was patented under the name Consuta.

In 1901 Saunders opened two works on the Isle of Wight; one at Whippingham for the manufacture of Consuta and the other at Cowes for the production and design of high speed motorboats. In 1912, it moved to a new yard on the west bank of the River Medina, known as Columbine. This move and the capital provided at the same time by the Wolseley Tool & Motor Car Company helped Sam Saunders to establish the firm of SE Saunders.

In the years before the First World War, Saunders produced a succession of racing motorboats including one named Ursula and in 1912 the British international Trophy award winner Maple Leaf IV. In 1909, it used Consuta in aircraft construction for the first time and two years later, produced gondolas for the naval airship Mayfly. Then, in 1912, it achieved further success with the construction of a flying boat hull for T & M Sopwith. This aircraft became the world's first successful seaplane.

In 1915, the company began aircraft production on the Isle of Wight after the receipt of a sub-contract for the construction of 50 AVRO 504A trainer aircraft and 30 Short 184 seaplanes. The company went on to produce a total of 201 AVRO 504s and 80 Short 184 seaplanes.

During this contract, Saunders continued to carry out experimental work on flying boats resulting in the eventual construction of 100 Porte-Felixstowe F2A flying boats and 50 of the later F5 model. Success in the world of aircraft production did however come at the expense of the ship building business.

Director and general manager, Walter Browning, 1954.

Saunders-Roe

At the end of the First World War the company received orders for the reconditioning of flying boats and de Havilland DH9A bombers. To cope with this increased workload a further new factory, the Osbourne Plymouth Works, was built for the manufacture of plywood while the Cowes works was expanded specifically for aircraft construction.

In 1918, the company also received additional sub-contract work following Vickers efforts to secure a 50 per cent share in the company. However, the work ended in 1921 after Sam Saunders bought out both Vickers and Wolsley and became the sole owner of SE Saunders Ltd.

Despite the company's joint aviation success, Sam Saunders wanted to design and manufacture his own aircraft. In 1917, the first of these was completed and despite financial constraints in the 1920s the company developed further successful designs for both land and seaplanes.

In 1925, there was an unsuccessful attempt to raise capital for these aviation projects and discussions were held with firms that included Swan, Hunter, Wigham Richardson Ltd and William Beardmore Ltd. The company also approached Vickers in a bid to establish a joint Vickers-Saunders aircraft production unit. Saunders were unable to accept Vickers terms however and that venture was abandoned.

Despite these setbacks the company was able to survive by focussing once again on boat building which had restarted on the island after the First World War. In 1929, it completed a commission to build the high powered craft Miss England II. Commissioned by Sir Henry Seagrave, it successfully reached a speed of 98.2mph before Sir Henry and his mechanic were killed during an attempt to break the world water speed record.

In 1936, the firm was thrust into the speed record spotlight once more when Sir Malcolm Campbell broke the world water speed record in the famous Saunders-built boat Bluebird. Two years later, it followed this success by producing an altogether slower vehicle in the form of its first river bus for use on the Thames. The vessel, named Pride of Westminster, provided a service between Westminster Bridge and Southend. It was a successful forerunner of the river buses that would provide regular services in later years. While Saunders' boat-building interests remained financially successful, its aircraft enterprise failed to maintain a profitable existence. Because of this, in 1928, the company invited Sir Alliott Verdon Roe and his associate, John Lord, to manage it. Fortunately both were fascinated by flying boat construction and had sold their previous interests in the AVRO Company.

The changes led to the formation of a new board of directors. Sam Saunders was appointed honorary president while Sir Alliott Verdon Roe and John Lord became joint managing directors; Mr. HF Broadsmith, general manager while messrs Hubert and Sam Saunders, Captain Nicholson and Mr. RV Prefect, who was appointed sales director in 1941, became directors, with Mr. Henry Knowler as chief engineer.

Further changes occurred in 1929 and the company was renamed Saunders-Roe Ltd, later abbreviated to Saro Ltd. At this point the Aircraft Investment Corporation acquired a financial stake in the company and in 1930, Whitehall Securities Corporation Ltd followed suit, obtaining a controlling interest. A new board of Saro directors was formed which included Captain HH Balfour PC, MC. He later became Lord Balfour of Inchrye, and during the years between 1938 and 1944 was promoted to the position of Under Secretary of State for Air.

During the 1930s, a new metal covering replaced the wood-based Consuta covering, traditionally used in the construction of flying boat hulls and floats. Soon after, in

An advertisement for Saunders-Roe Ltd which appeared in The Aeroplane magazine on November 25, 1936.

**This aerial view of the Beaumaris factory while under the ownership
of Cammell Laird (Anglesey) Ltd shows its close proximity to the sea.**

1936, production of the Lerwick flying boat began. Three years later, the company built a one-quarter scale flying boat for use as a flying test bed. This scaled down craft tested many of the features later used in the Short/Saro designed and built boat, the Shetland.

Before and after the First World War, the company continued to build lifeboats for the Royal National Lifeboat Institution. However, production of these stopped in 1933 when Sam Saunders died and his son Hubert resigned from the board. As a result of Hubert's resignation the board passed control of the lifeboat building business to the firm of Graves and Gutteridge.

In 1936, the Cowes factory experienced further expansion including the provision of a new hanger on the Medina site. This became famous in the post-war years as the backdrop for many of the company's promotional aircraft photographs. One memorable image portrays Princess flying boats set against the front of the hanger proudly displaying the Saunders-Roe name.

In 1937, the company once again expanded its production facilities with the purchase of a factory in Eastleigh. In addition, negotiations were started for the purchase of a small North Wales estate, one mile north of the town of Beaumaris on the Isle of Anglesey that was the site of the Fryars country house.

The decision to buy the estate showed remarkable foresight, for during the summer of 1940, the Ministry of Aircraft Production awarded Saunders-Roe the contract to carry out modifications to Consolidated Catalina flying boats. The contract also included the production of drawings and the manufacturing of parts. The Catalina flying boats were due to enter service with the Royal Air Force after their arrival from the United States. Rather than delay their arrival by modifying the aircraft on the production line, the decision was taken to modify them once delivery had taken place.

The Beaumaris factory was ideally located for the trial installations. Without a doubt, the waters of the Menai Strait, north of the Telford Suspension Bridge, provided the ideal stretch of sheltered water required to trial and manage the flying boats. In addition, the house within the estate provided suitable space for the factory's offices.

During the post war years, the company used the Catalina flying boat contract to create the factory's telegraphic address — Seaboats. The name was later altered to Searoads, reflecting the change in the factory's products.

In 1938, Saunders-Roe established another new business at Whippingham. Saro Laminated Wood Products Ltd became responsible for producing 40 per cent of the aircraft plywood used in the British Isles. The factory was also known for manufacturing other items including doors and trolley bus roofs. Many of its panels were also used extensively within the building and shipbuilding industries. Later, some of them were used on London Underground trains and other railway rolling stock.

The continual pressure of the company's aircraft associated work resulted in the building of another new yard for its boat building. Named Saunders Shipyard Ltd it concentrated

On July 27, 1939 Flight magazine carried this advertisement for Saro Laminated Wood Products Ltd.

An advertisement for the Saro Skeeter helicopter which appeared in *The Aeroplane* magazine on June 20, 1952.

on the production of special sectioned tugs for the Admiralty until it was destroyed by enemy action during 1942.

After the outbreak of the Second World War, production of the Walrus flying boat was transferred to Saro. This decision enabled Vickers-Supermarine to focus on production of the famous Spitfire fighter aircraft. At a later date, Sea Otter production was also transferred to Saro. By the end of the war, it had built a total of 461 Walrus and 291 Sea Otter aircraft.

In response to the increased war effort, Saro was forced to continually move and expand. In 1940, it relocated its head office to Melchett Court in Romsey, Hampshire. However, the design team were moved to safety in Beaumaris until the end of the war. The company also established new factories in Weybridge, Surrey and sub-contract work for Fairey Aviation was undertaken in Hersham and Byfleet. The company's interest in the Weybridge factory ceased in 1946.

Saro's war effort also brought changes to its management structure. In 1937, Captain ED Clark was appointed commercial director. Two years later, he was promoted to joint managing director and then, in 1945, managing director, a post he held until he resigned following a takeover of the company in 1960.

In 1943, Arthur Gouge of Short Brothers became vice-chairman of Saro. Later knighted, the famous Short Sunderland flying boat designer provided the company with inspiration in its determination to produce a design for the Short Saro Shetland flying boat. The company hoped that this boat would later replace the Short Sunderland design.

In 1944, it decided to build a prototype Shetland. However, two years later, the aircraft was destroyed by fire at its mooring in Cowes. Despite this setback, a second prototype was built and flown before the project was finally abandoned in 1949.

In 1945, the firm decided to establish the Saunders Shipyard Company at the former aircraft factory in Beaumaris. Geoffrey Verdon Roe was appointed managing director while the Hon. HP Morgan Granville OBE took on the role of chairman at Saro Ltd. In addition, Walter Browning, formerly a director of the company, became its general manager in 1946.

During the post war years, the company's head office was relocated to 153 Parliament Street, Westminster, London, before moving to 45 Parliament Street. After the war, work still continued at the Eastleigh factory and under sub-contract, a number of assemblies were produced for designs including: the de Havilland Venom and the Supermarine Swift and Scimitar and Vickers Viscount aircraft. At the same time, it also manufactured parts for the SR/A1 fighter and the three Princess flying boats.

In 1951, a helicopter division was formed at Eastleigh following the manufacture, under licence, of the Italian Cierva Autogire helicopter designs. Previously, SE Saunders had built a form of the Autogyro known as a helicogyre to the design of Vittorio Isacco. The Skeeter was the first design produced by the company's new

This image of work under way on the SR.45 Princess Flying Boat was part of an
advertisement which appeared in The Aeroplane magazine on October 29, 1948.

division. The aircraft was used by the armies of both Britain and the Federal Republic of Germany. In 1957 a five-seat helicopter design known as the Saro 531 was developed. It was flown for the first time in 1958 and later became known as the Westland Wasp or Scout.

During 1956, following the sub-contract work at Eastleigh, de Havilland Holdings purchased a 33 per cent shareholding in Saro. Later, this influence resulted in the division's production of rocket engines for Britain's Blue Streak missile and also a Black Knight research rocket that was tested at Woomera, Australia.

During the post war years, the Cowes factory continued the company's interest in the production of innovative flying boat designs. In 1947, it flew the world's first flying boat fighter, the SR/A1, This aircraft was designed in addition to the giant flying boat SR45, which later became known as the Princess flying boat.

The SR45 was created with the BOAC airline in mind. Capable of carrying 200 passengers, it was powered by 10 Bristol Proteus gas turbine engines and weighed 120 tons. The company produced three of these although only one of them flew — in August 1952 — and after initial testing the craft was deemed underpowered.

Four years later, the company's plan to produce large-scale flying boats was finally brought to an end. In October 1950, BOAC decided to close down the flying boat services it had established before the start of the Second World War. Two years later, in May 1952, the launch of the de Havilland Comet jet airliner effectively ended the glory days of the flying boat.

For the following 12 years, the three Princess flying boats were stored at Calshot and Cowes. Various schemes were considered for their use including a proposal to re-engine them with Rolls Royce Tyne turbo-prop units. However, this never materialised and they were eventually sold for scrap in 1965 and 1967.

Despite this setback the company continued to move forward and created an interceptor fighter, the SR53. A rocket engine was used to power this advanced aircraft and elements of its design were later developed in the SR177. Interestingly, the jet powered SR177 featured the use of rocket motors powered by High Test Peroxide for which Saunders also built road transport tankers.

Ignoring interest from abroad, reductions in the defence expenditure during the 1960s resulted in the termination of the advanced fighter project. The failure of the Princess flying boat and the SR177 fighter to go into production proved a great disappointment to the company.

During its final years, the direction of the business changed. In 1957, a civil engineering company, Saro Structures, was formed to produce light alloy structures. Two years later, the company developed an association with Nuclear Enterprises (GB) Ltd, of Edinburgh which was formed to explore the use of isotopes within industrial processes. In 1957, the Cowes factory secured a contract to build a hovercraft. Two years later, during May, 1959, its SRN 1 became the first Hovercraft to emerge from the factory in Cowes.

Within a year of Sir Alliott Verdon Roe's death in 1958, Sir Arthur Gouge retired as Saro's chief executive. In August 1959, Westland Aircraft, a member of the Hawker Siddeley group, absorbed the Saro helicopter division and production was transferred from Cowes to Yeovil in Somerset. After the takeover, the Cowes factory became known as the Saunders-Roe Division of Westland Aircraft Ltd. However, hovercraft production continued under the factory's new owners at Cowes. Finally, in March 1994, the GKN Group took control of Westland Aircraft Ltd.

This drawing of the giant Saunders-Roe hanger at East Cowes, Isle of Wight, was often used in company advertising.
This full page example appeared in The Aeroplane magazine on November 25, 1936.

C.Z.C.MORTON

SAUNDERS-ROE LTD.
EAST COWES - - ISLE OF WIGHT

By Appointment.

Builders of the SARO CLOUD AMPHIBIANS used for navigational training

YOUR LETTERS TO ADVERTISERS SHOULD MENTION "THE AEROPLANE."

Anglesey arrival

In 1940, Saunders-Roe was awarded a Ministry of Aircraft production contract to convert consolidated Catalina flying boats to the Royal Air Force's requirements. Wartime hostilities with Germany were increasing and the factory at Cowes was vulnerable to enemy attack. As a result, a decision was taken to transfer the Catalina work and the design staff to the company's new factory in Beaumaris.

However, the company faced a significant problem. At Beaumaris, the slipway used to draw the aircraft out of the water and the factory were both still under construction. So instead, the Catalinas were flown to Greenock on the River Clyde after their Transatlantic crossing. On their arrival, the firm arranged to use Scottish Aviation's Caird's Yard for the conversion work. A small group of design staff were sent to Scotland to start the modification process while the new Beaumaris factory was completed.

The first Catalina arrived at the Scottish yard in February 1941, For a while, work progressed until, in May of that year, the site was bombed by the Luftwaffe. In addition, the level of conversion work had risen beyond the yard's capacity and a decision was taken to transfer it to the newly-built Beaumaris factory. The first aircraft arrived in North Wales in July 1941.

Initially, conversion was carried out while the aircraft were kept afloat. Eventually, the completion of the new slipway enabled them to be drawn out of the water and brought into the hanger for the required modification.

By 1942, the level of work had increased dramatically and the factory became known locally as the US Aircraft Department. Although much of the modification work remained secret, the contract included the fitting of anti-submarine radar. In addition, American-made submarine tracking equipment was fitted to later aircraft destined for use by the RAF's Coastal Command. From November 1942, aircraft sent to Beaumaris were no longer required to land at Greenock and instead were flown direct to Beaumaris from Bermuda.

During the war, various types of aircraft were seen in the Menai Strait including the Vought-Sikorsky Kingfisher, Short Sunderlands, Consolidated Catalina flying boats, Fairey Seafox, Spitfire Floatplane, Curtis Seamew, Martin Mariner and the consolidated Coronado flying boats. In addition, trial work was undertaken in

Beaumaris on a one-quarter scale flying boat used in the design of the new Short Saro Shetland aircraft.

After the war, the Ministry of Defence ended the modification programme and in June 1945 advised Saunders-Roe to complete all work in hand. As a result, the company's design staff moved back to Cowes and in September that year, the Beaumaris factory was closed. This presented a problem for the management of Saro. Located within an area of high unemployment, the factory's employees would struggle to find alternative work. In order to retain the workforce, a decision was made to relocate the Saunders Shipyard Company to Beaumaris. This was instigated on September 13, 1945 and resulted in changes to the board of directors. Three new members were appointed: WP Kemp as managing director; PD Irons and A Gouge. On appointment to his new role, PD Irons relinquished the post of company secretary which he had held since November 21, 1944. He was replaced by RJ Sargeant until May 3, 1947 when he resigned, and Irons was reappointed company secretary in addition to his directorship.

Following the emergence of the new board it was decided to change the company's name. The factory was no longer primarily concerned with shipbuilding and the existing name failed to take into account its engineering work and the production of public service vehicle bodywork. As a result, on January 11, 1946, the company became Saunders Engineering & Shipyard Ltd.

In 1947, REW Holmes became sales director. Following his early training with Park Royal and AEC Ltd at Southall, Middlesex, Holmes had a distinguished war career before returning as a member of the AEC salesforce. With Saunders, his knowledge

Two trolleybuses are towed across the Menai Bridge in the rain by Leyland Motors trucks on the first stage of their long delivery journey to Auckland, New Zealand, on September 30, 1954.

Five AEC Regents destined for Durban nearing completion alongside two Bristol double deck vehicles being built for Maidstone & District.

and experience proved invaluable in its quest to manufacture public service vehicle bodywork. Mr Holmes retained his post until the production of bodywork at Beaumaris ended. Following home and overseas appointments, he later became sales director of AEC.

For a well-known ship building company, Saunders' decision to produce public service vehicle bodywork may seem unusual. However, other firms including Short Bros. had already undertaken similar work following the end of the First World War, when faced with a reduced demand for aircraft, the company was forced to find other ways to retain their skilled workforce. In 1920, production of vehicle bodywork began at its Rochester factory. As demand for its products increased so the company became a major supplier of single and double deck bodywork for trams and road vehicles.

Short Bros. supplied bodywork to a number of bus operators including London General, Birmingham Corporation, East Kent, Maidstone & District, Birmingham & Midland Motor Omnibus Company, Southdown, Northern General, Devon General and Western SMT. Some of the same operators later received bodywork from Beaumaris. An increase in aircraft production during the early 1930's saw Short Bros. withdraw from vehicle bodywork production in 1935.

The decision by Saunders to build bodywork was no surprise, particularly as some of its directors, including WP Kemp, had previously been associated with Short Bros.

The fast patrol boat Dark Aggressor launches torpedos as it is put through its paces.

The experimental aluminium yacht Morag Mhor.

and familiar with such activities. However, it was the intervention of nature that eventually led to the realisation of the dream to build bus bodies.

In 1944, high winds caused serious structural problems to the Telford Suspension Bridge across the Menai Strait. Opened in 1826, it carried the only road link across the Menai Strait and with it the main A5 trunk road to Holyhead. Before the advent of railways, the bridge reduced the length of time horse-drawn coaches took to carry the Irish mail to and from London. It wasn't, however, designed to take the weight of road vehicles exceeding 4 tons 5 cwt.

Following representations from, among others, Crosville Motor Services, Caernarvonshire County Council agreed to rebuild the bridge and increase the loading to allow the passage of heavier road vehicles, including double deck buses. The decision pleased everyone concerned, including Crosville who maintained a batch of lightweight buses in order to provide services to and from Anglesey. Beaumaris factory employees assisted in the repair and alteration of the bridge and in March 1945, the first double deck bus crossed over the bridge. As a result, the factory was able to start refurbishing and producing bodywork for public service vehicles.

Boats not buses were still the main focus of the factory's labours at this time, however, and although the wartime flying boat slipway was still available for use, this necessitated the construction of a new one capable of launching vessels weighing up to 300 tons. When complete it featured a cradle running along a track and enabled vessels to be launched directly into the Menai Strait.

One of the 40 Bristol K6As delivered to Maidstone & District between May and September, 1948.

The factory's Cecostamp drop hammer formed a variety of components such as door panels, rear quarter panels and window pans.

Many folding operations were carried out on large brake presses such as the one being operated by this employee.

Large panels were rapidly cut to the required contour by a Pullomax machine seen in use above.

Work underway on roof parcel racks which were completed as separate assemblies and fitted to the body immediately after erection.

One of the typical sub-assemblies was the front crib member. This load was being taken to the stores.

Royal Tiger chassis for Cuba are being fitted with floors, while three single deck bodies on Daimler CVD chassis are awaiting completion for Kumasi. The double deck body is mounted on an AEC Regent III chassis that was later registered as OKM 317. In the background construction of a number of pontoons is underway.

During the immediate post war years, the Admiralty awarded Saunders a contract to design and build the world's first all aluminium alloy motor torpedo boat. In 1948, the company also completed the first of several other boats for the Royal Navy. Later, between June and December 1952, the factory constructed other vessels for the Royal Navy including a number of 106ft long minesweepers. Three were of all wood construction and four of aluminium alloy frames clad with wood.

In October 1954, Saunders launched its first Dark class fast patrol boat named Dark Adventure. The Beaumaris factory went on to supply further similar vessels to the Royal Navy as well as the governments of Burma, Finland and Japan. In 1954, it was commissioned to build an all-aluminium alloy 72ft auxiliary yacht for the British Aluminium Company. Used mainly for demonstration purposes, the Morag Mhor became the first vessel ever to be built using large scale Argon Arc welded aluminium in its construction.

The introduction of a test tank facility enabled the company to continue producing innovative hull designs. Among these, in 1957, was the hydrofoil Bras d'Or. Following its launch, the tanks were used to test hulls for America's Cup challengers.

The company continued to develop the use of aluminium alloy and used the technology to build a lightweight lifeboat for use in air-sea rescue work. This was designed for carriage under the fuselage of Avro Shackleton aircraft and could be released from the air into the sea without suffering damage.

The same material was used to produce portable bridges for the Army. Specialist work using aluminium alloy was also undertaken to produce torpedo launchers and diving decompression chambers for various Royal Navy contracts.

At a later date, the company experimented with laminated woods in boat building. These were used for the fabrication of hull frames and the necessary machines and ovens were all installed in the factory.

During the 1950's, Saunders utilised another innovative material within the manufacturing process. Glass reinforced fibres were used to make ventilator units and the production of 18ft long general purpose dinghies. However, it wasn't long before this process was also being used in the manufacture of shaped panels for the Saro single deck bus body.

Full scale plans promoted accuracy and reduced the chances of errors in detail design.

The one-off fibreglass body fitted to a Land Rover 4 x 4 forward control chassis in 1954.

In 1954, a fibreglass body was built for a forward control 4x4 Land Rover chassis. Although this remained the only example, the company continued other experimental work including Land Rovers fitted with rear traction drives.

In addition to new contracts, the factory undertook work to repair rafts and timber bridging equipment for the Army. Despite the decline in the production of public service vehicle bodywork, it continued to produce specialist vehicle bodies for the armed forces including some mounted on Commer Superpoise 4x4 chassis.

Among other road related products, the Beaumaris factory built trailer-mounted High Test Peroxide storage tanks for the military. However, the most unusual product to emerge from there must surely have been the front housing for the English Electric experimental turbine railway locomotive GT3 in 1957. The aluminium alloy housing carried the turbine air intake filters, oil filters and turbine starter motor.

Saunders' expertise in the use of aluminium alloys and associated welding techniques also enabled it to produce body designs for road tankers. It manufactured a number of fuel tanker bodies that were fitted onto a variety of heavy goods vehicle chassis for petrol companies and the military.

In 1955, the factory built two specialised road tankers, mounted on eight-wheel AEC Mammoth Major Mark III chassis. Capable of towing a two-axle trailer, each tanker was designed to carry High Test Peroxide, a fuel used to power Saro's rocket-engined fighter SR53, the SR177 fighter and the Blue Streak missile. The first completed

A Leyland Comet articulated lorry loaded with the front nose section of the English Electric gas turbine locomotive GT3.

vehicle appeared on display at the 1955 Farnborough Air Show. Following the company's success, the factory received orders from Shell-BP for tankers mounted on Atkinson eight-wheel and AEC Mercury 4x2 chassis. Esso Aviation services ordered tanks mounted on Bedford 4x2 chassis while the military took delivery of aircraft refuelling tanks mounted on 6x4 Leyland Hippo chassis. In 1959 however, the production of the Yorkshire class aircraft refueller for Air-BP surpassed Saunder's previous road refuelling tanker designs. The pumping and control equipment were mounted on an AEC Mammoth Major Mark III 6x2 chassis used to tow a 10,000 gallon articulated tanker. The vehicle was designed to provide fuel for the large jet airliners entering service at that time including the Boeing 707 and the de Havilland Comet. The vehicle was, in its day the largest capacity road tanker in the world.

In January 1951, the company's name was changed to Saunders-Roe (Anglesey) Ltd. This was retained until it was sold to de Havilland Holdings and became Saro

The HTP tank mounted on an AEC Mammoth Major Mark III chassis with the trailer carrying a water tank.

(Anglesey) Ltd. The de Havilland Holdings company formed part of the Hawker Siddeley group which included the Westland Aircraft Company and Gloster Aircraft, based in Gloucestershire. During 1963-4, the company once again changed its name, this time to Gloster-Saro in response to the merger of the two tank manufacturing businesses. Around 1967, the Beaumaris factory was sold to the Laird Group and the company renamed Cammell Laird (Anglesey) Ltd. Interestingly, the Laird Group also owned Birmingham-based bus builders MCW. The factory's new owners agreed to build a German company's product under licence. This entailed constructing bodies for refuse collection vehicles mounted on a variety of lorry chassis. In 1968, the first Shark refuse collection body was completed at Beaumaris.

The same year, the factory restarted production of public service vehicle bodywork after a 10 year break. It received orders to produce two batches of MCW designed bodywork, mounted on Leyland Titan and Atlantean chassis. The Brighton Corporation and Devon General orders were produced at Beaumaris in an effort to reduce pressure on MCW's Birmingham factory. At the time, it was heavily committed to the production of bodywork for London Transport vehicles.

During the 1960s, the Superior Coach Company of America granted a licence for MCW to assemble and supply the company's single deck body design. The body was

A Shark refuse collection body mounted on a Leyland Clydesdale chassis and fitted with a crew cab.

Some of the staff in the production control department during the heyday of bus building at Beaumaris.

supplied to the UK as a completely knocked down (CKD) kit for use in the UK and Europe. The first body kit was assembled on a Ford chassis in Birmingham and the results were shown to the Beaumaris factory's management in June 1968. As a result, further body kits were assembled at Beaumaris on Bedford and Ford chassis during 1968 and 1969. These were to be the last passenger carrying bodies built at the factory.

In November 1970, the company's name changed to Laird (Anglesey) Ltd. In addition to its existing range of products, it now began producing trackway systems for use in locations requiring access or temporary aircraft runways. It also designed and manufactured loading terminals for use in the busy JFK, New York, Bahrain and Shannon Airports.

During the 1970s, while production of the Shark refuse collection vehicles continued. The firm developed a design for what became the Rotopress refuse collection vehicle. The design became popular with many local authorities and private companies during a time when wheeled refuse containers came into use for the collection of household and commercial refuse.

In later years, the company followed this success and manufactured the Variomatic body under licence. Finally, the purchase of the Telstar range of road gritting bodies increased the company's portfolio of utility bodies. Local authorities and government agencies used these vehicles to keep the road network open during icy winter weather. For many people, the Beaumaris factory will be remembered not only for its products but also the company's innovative approach to production and design. During the

A Vario-Press refuse collection body fitted to a three axle Seddon Atkinson chassis complete with a crew cab.

early 1950s, the factory site occupied around 28.5 acres and utilised approximately 240,000 square feet of covered floor space. At the height of public service vehicle bodywork production, 100,000 square feet of this was used to produce bodywork providing employment for more than seven hundred people. Amazingly, the factory's entire production was contained within the buildings and the company was able to adjust the factory's floor space to suit any particular need.

Design and build

Most manufacturers of public service vehicle coachwork incorporate distinctive features within their body designs. Down the years the use of raised waist rails in the Charles Roe (Leeds) bodies or the characteristic dorsal fin ventilator fitted at the rear of Harrington coach bodies, are prime examples. Sometimes, the external shape of the body can also distinguish one design from another. For Saunders, the evolution of such distinctive features took longer to achieve and it was the arrival of the Rivaloy body that was to mark the appearance of the first definitive Saunders' design.

During the early years of production at Beaumaris between 1946 and 1949, most single and double deck bodies were based on the designs of the pre-war Short Bros. Company. Many of the Short-built bodies were largely constructed from wood and produced in the traditional manner. They also used metal as frame re-enforcement, complete with external cladding.

In 1928 Shorts produced some experimental designs using metal for body framing. The company also built an aluminium body employing the techniques of aircraft construction. Subsequently, an aluminium-framed body using H sections was supplied to Birmingham Corporation on a tram under-frame.

Shorts continued work on developing a metal body and in 1934 completed a design for a new double deck body. The first six examples of this were supplied to the Western Scottish Motor Traction Company, mounted on Leyland Titan chassis. Of these buses, three lowbridge versions were operated by Greenock Motor Services, a subsidiary company, while the highbridge or normal height buses were placed in the Western SMT's own fleet.

The framing for these bodies originated from a design created and patented by WP Kemp. This incorporated a high tensile, steel cruciform section pillar and simplified the construction of the body framing. It reduced the need to use plates where the sections came together and made the section strong enough to resist both lateral and longitudinal stress. The completed frame was further strengthened with the fitment of sheet steel pressings. In order to reduce the weight, holes were cut into the sheets and the pressings were fitted at the waist rail, front bulkhead and rear wheel arches of the body. The exterior and interior panels were fixed to the frame pillars by screws driven into wooden blocks and bolted onto the pillar sections. Viewed from the end, this resembled a cross with uniform arms. The ledges formed by the arms allowed the wooden blocks to be located, drilled and bolted to each other through the arm of the pillar section, sandwiched between the blocks. Finally, wire cables were used to transmit the stresses within the body framing to the front and rear bulkhead.

In 1935, a front entrance, aluminium framed version of this double deck body was designed for the Birmingham & Midland Motor Omnibus Company (BMMO). However, because of the closure of the factory, it was never built. Saunders' use of aluminium alloys in vehicle bodies was by no means unique. At the end of the 1940s, a number of coachbuilders were using this material for the construction of bodywork including Beadle, Harrington, Seddon, Strachans and Dutfield. Eastern Coachworks also used aluminium alloy in a large part of their design for a new body and in September 1949, Scottish Aviation produced a mainly aluminium alloy 56 seat double deck body. This was mounted on a Foden PVD6 chassis and weighed 2 tons 13 cwt 2 qrs. Scottish Aviation was associated with Saunders-Roe during the war and several years later after Scottish Aviation embarked on coachbuilding, Saunders-Roe produced a double deck body design approximately 15 cwt lighter.

Jig-built body sides being assembled onto an ACLO Regal chassis as part of the Argentinian order.

Three very different products of the Beaumaris factory lined up outside Fryars in 1968. They are, from left to right: a Superior bodied Bedford VAM, Shark refuse collection vehicle and a Devon General Atlantean fleet number 540.

At Beaumaris, a team of designers worked under the leadership of the chief engineer, CE Butterfield. Many of their final designs incorporated his innovative ideas. However, much care was also taken in the selection of materials for bodywork construction. These were selected for their strength and corrosion resistance. The British Aluminium Company supplied most of the aluminium alloy and many of the sections were produced to the requirements of Saunders-Roe.

Before Saunders-Roe could embark on large-scale production, the drawings and patterns were laid out in full size inside the factory's draughting loft. Originally, this

Two lines of single deck bodies being built on Guy Arab chassis destined for Holland using traditional methods.

Leyland Tiger Cub chassis being bodied for Yorkshire Traction. Completed roof sections are stacked up alongside.

facility was designed to allow ship designers to set out their hull drawings. It also enabled the company to reduce production errors and ensure drilled holes lined up when the parts came together on the assembly lines.

In order to test the soundness of the designs, the design team used the Motor Industry Research Association's test ground at Lindley, near Nuneaton. Opened in 1949, the company used the former airfield to test the early Saunders Bodies including the first Rivaloy single deck body. The body, constructed on a Leyland Royal Tiger chassis, was destined for use in Cuba. As a condition of this contract, all testing had to be successfully completed before any production could commence.

In 1951, the testing ground facilities were enhanced with the addition of a Belgian pave section and corrugated tracks. These facilities proved beneficial when the team tested the lightweight, aluminium double deck body mounted on an AEC Regent Mark III chassis.

During the test, body fittings including seats and interior lining panels were removed from the body. Instead, measuring devices were installed to record the stresses and strains as the vehicle moved over the pave and corrugated tracks. Under these conditions 10 days of testing were equivalent to around 500, 000 miles of normal service and equated to the designed lifespan of the body. The company also used the Motor Industry Research Association's facilities to test the body designs supplied to

An ACLO Regal III chassis carries its body framing prior to panelling. The cross-braced cruciform pillars are clearly visible. The front wings were extended below the bottom of the radiator.

Double deck bodies for Maidstone & District under construction. Two upper deck assemblies are being built on the floor while the background vehicle reveals the rear wheel arch stress panel lightening holes.

the Argentinian and Kumasi clients. Other products tested in this way included the prototype Saro single deck body fitted to a Leyland Tiger Cub chassis and the integral single deck bus design. Great care was taken to ensure bodies were well proven and able to offer a long, economical operating life before they went into full production.

Single deck bodies

All bodywork supplied on AEC, Guy and Foden chassis had frames formed using metal cruciform pillar sections. The roof sticks or frames were also constructed from aluminium. The methods used to accommodate stresses within these bodies varied with each group produced. Northern General bodywork, for example, was built to BET Federation standard single deck design. This involved sheet steel stress panels containing weight reduction holes used at floor level and positioned over the rear wheel arches.

After a short period of service however, the lack of stress panels at waist rail level was considered the main cause of a high degree of body movement. As a result, all the bodies were returned to Beaumaris for rectification work.

The company increased the number of stress panels used for bodies built on Foden, Guy and AEC chassis for the Lisbon order. Again, panels were added at waist rail level and holes were drilled to reduce the weight. However, the bodywork produced for Holland featured bearers manufactured from pressed sections. Once more, holes were drilled throughout the length of these to reduce weight. The bearers were used to fix the body to the Guy chassis frame and match the position of the side pillars.

Eventually, the company adopted a fresh approach to tackle the issue of body stress control. Work on the order for the Argentinian contract involved the design of

An AEC Regal Mark III vehicle destined for Lisbon.

One of the left hand drive, long wheel-based Guy Arab Mark III chassis supplied to operators in Holland.

bodywork mounted on an AEC chassis. In the body frame, pressed sheet steel stress panels were replaced with cruciform pillar sections placed diagonally between the main pillars. The body framing design consisted of five parts: the two body sides, the roof, the rear end and the front bulkhead. Importantly, these were the first bodies to be produced using jigs at Beaumaris. They were also the first bodies to be constructed from units, the forerunner of the later Rivaloy design.

Double deck bodies

The first three orders for the company's double deck bodywork were supplied to a plan based on the 1934 Short Bros. design. This included the cruciform steel pillar and contained lightened sheet steel stress panels. A steel cable was also used to transfer stress to the front and rear body bulkheads. In keeping with normal practice, the double deck bodies were built in two halves. The lower deck frame was built directly onto the chassis while the upper deck frame was erected on the factory floor and then lifted onto the lower deck frame to complete the body.

All the bodies supplied to London Transport were manufactured using the same methods. However, the body framing was built in jigs especially made for the purpose. Before being fitted to the chassis, the lower deck frame was erected in such a jig. This enabled the company to produce exactly the same body frame each time.

The bodies supplied to London Transport by Saunders differed from those of main contractors Park Royal and Weymann. Saunders used the cruciform pillar section in place of both contractors preference for interior stress panels and channel sections positioned at waist rail level. Also, the Park Royal and Weymann Jicwood roof were not incorporated in the Saunders bodywork which allowed the upper deck roofs to be built in the normal way.

RT PRODUCTION

Single deck Rivaloy bodies

The Saunders design for the single deck body was based on the bodywork constructed for Argentina and Brazil. However, the use of aluminium alloy H-sections marked a change in the material used to construct the body side framing. The internal and external panels were normally riveted to the frame. Screws were used when operators wanted to assemble the body in their own workshops. Increasingly, the main components of the body were also assembled in jigs. The window pans, glazing, interior and exterior panels were fitted before the body was lowered onto the chassis.

The first Rivaloy bodies, built on vertical front-engined chassis, consisted of four main units: the roof, the two sides and the rear. The sections were bolted together on the steel under-frame which was erected directly onto the chassis. The body sections were bolted together because each unit possessed a facing member formed from an aluminium alloy U-section, built into various parts of the individual sections. The channel sections in the roof and end units were drilled and fitted with captive nuts. In order to allow the fixing bolts to pass through, sections were also drilled in the body sides.

When assembled, the window finishers covered the fixing bolts in the body sides and cover strips were placed along the body side. In addition, the body's interior finish

A lower deck RT body assembly is built up on a jig.

Lower deck frame assemblies in the process of being fitted to London RT chassis.

The lower deck frame jig and the upper deck side frame jigs are positioned in the hanger ready for production. Double deck bodies on Bristol chassis for Maidstone & District can be seen in the background. On the right the three AEC Regals fitted with front bumpers were destined for Lisbon.

reflected the influence of the London Transport RT design. For example, the company used window cappings of a half round design secured with polished strips located at the joints.

Chassis incorporating a full front required small changes within their design. The bodymaker no longer needed the supplied chassis bulkhead, located in front of the driver and therefore, a new front was required. Full fronts were incorporated within the bodywork supplied to Argentina and Brazil.

For the Brazilian order, ideas gleaned from the practices of other South American coachbuilders were used in the construction of experimental front assemblies. One of the mock-up fronts featured a very rounded, deep front dome together with a recessed, flat driver's windscreen. Eventually, this formed the basis for the new frontal design used on all subsequent Rivaloy bodies mounted on front and under-floor chassis.

The first examples of the new design appeared on the two bodies built on the Commer Avenger chassis. In addition, the company used a slightly modified version of this design on the later Saro single deck body. This became a very distinctive feature of the Saunders-Roe design. However, another feature also appeared for the first time on the two Commer bodies. The company fitted a lifeguard rail at the bottom of the body side panels, inset at the front, just behind the front wheels.

For under-floor engined chassis, the Rivaloy body design was further modified to incorporate the use of six main units. These units: the two sides, the roof, the front and rear ends together with the floor, were built directly onto the chassis frame. The floor unit also incorporated bodyside mounting points and these were used in conjunction with the chassis outriggers. This method of assembly allowed the body to be sent overseas in a partially knocked down (PKD) condition.

London Transport RT double deck buses alongside single deck vehicles bound for Sao Paulo, Brazil, on line at Beaumaris in 1949. From left to right, the RT's are numbers 1199, 1204 and 1198.

To save space, and with it, shipping costs, Saunders devised a method of packing the units onto the chassis. All the components for three complete buses were mounted onto three chassis. These were already fitted with a floor, complete with entry and exit steps and the wheel arch panels.

One of the chassis carried the body sides while another accommodated the roof units. The third was used to carry the front and rear ends. Internal fittings including the seats, handrails, light fittings and doors were packed into containers and fixed to the chassis, under the three roof sections.

In 1951 the company organised an event to demonstrate the simplicity of assembling a body in its PKD form, using the minimum of workshop equipment. It decided to assemble a body built for the Cuban contract in front of an invited audience which included members of the transport industry and technical press. Although the work

One of the designs for bodies mounted on vertical forward-engined chassis. The South American influence is clear and the front dome and sloping windscreen arrangement were intended for use with the Rivaloy body. The mock- up carried an ACLO radiator badge though the design wasn't used for bodies supplied on conventional chassis.

This design mock-up was attached to one of the bodies under construction for the Argentinian contract. It was not used although some of its design features were incorporated into bodies eventually built for Sao Paulo. The vehicle is parked between the staging being used at the time for the construction of RT double deck bodies.

would normally take sixty man hours, seven men assembled the body within six and a half hours. This demonstration body differed slightly from the normal production PKD version. It was finished externally in the livery of the operator rather than being supplied in primer. Once the bodywork was complete, the observers were invited to board the vehicle for an hour-long trip around Anglesey. The company later used the PKD system to export single deck bodywork to Cuba and New Zealand. Following the introduction of the Saro single deck design, it decided to modify the later Rivaloy single deck bodies. These changes enabled the saloon floor to be assembled independently. The completed bodyshell could then be lowered onto the chassis. Chobert pop rivets were also introduced into the construction process.

All the Rivaloy single deck designs were built from side frames. The body pillars were made from aluminium alloy and mounted onto a steel under-frame. The company also used steel for many parts including the roof sticks, wheel arch panels, waist rails, together with the front and rear domes. The internal stress panels, secured to the frame with solid rivets, were also steel. Although some of the contracts required sheet steel for the exterior side panels, most were made from aluminium. The company also used mild steel to make the front and rear domes on all the bodies. Not surprisingly, the name Rivaloy reflected the riveted-alloy body design.

Double deck Rivaloy bodies

Following the production of the single deck body, the design team at Beaumaris turned their attention to the creation of a new double deck version. The design incorporated the same principles as the single deck Rivaloy including an aluminium alloy frame mounted on a steel under-frame built onto the chassis. Externally, the new body was similar in appearance to the London Transport RT design and differed only in the use of a flatter front and deeper lower saloon side panels. Internally, it was also finished in the London style with rounded window cappings together with curved ceilings in both the lower and upper saloons. Some of the jigs used to build the London Transport bodies may also have been used to produce the new design.

In 1950, the first Rivaloy double deck body, mounted on a reconditioned Bristol K6A chassis, was produced for Maidstone & District Motor Services Ltd. In the following year, a lightweight version of the design, built entirely from aluminium alloy, was mounted on an AEC Regent Mark III chassis.

The body pillars formed the H-section while the upper deck floor was supported by a cross-braced structure. Bearers formed from pressed aluminium alloy sections were

The first assembly of Rivaloy single deck bodies on Leyland Tiger chassis for Crosville. The jigs used can be seen in the background.

Construction underway on a demonstration body on a Leyland Royal Tiger chassis for the Cuba contract.

A completed Rivaloy single deck body is lowered onto a Leyland Royal Tiger chassis bound for Auckland. The AEC gear change quadrant is attached to the steering column. The AEC pre-selector gearbox can also be seen.

riveted together to form a beam, attached to the side pillars and incorporated in the cross-braced structure. The under frame was built from aluminium alloy sections.

In 1952, the company built a third lightweight all-aluminium alloy double deck body which differed from previous Saunders designs. Designed to meet the requirements of Birmingham City Transport, it incorporated their standard design. Compared to the first all-alloy body design, fewer lightened beams and longitudinal supports were used within the construction of the upper deck floor.

Saro single deck body

In 1951, work started on the creation of a lightweight single deck bus body, based on the Rivaloy design. This was intended for use on the new range of lightweight under-floor engined chassis being developed around the same time. Created to reduce weight, the design featured panels instead of horizontal rails behind the main pillars.

For strength these panels were folded along their length. The roof and side panels were also used to provide longtitudinal strength. The internal stress panels, riveted to the pillars, were folded in such a way that the seats could be directly fixed to them. This process enabled the assemblers to dispense with the rail normally fitted along the sides of the body.

In keeping with the Rivaloy design, the company wanted to build the body in sections. However, the design included one important modification. At floor level, a special aluminium section was incorporated into the body sides. This was known as the crib rail and was used to locate the main pillars to the floor-chassis mounting points. The feature also enabled Saunders to use a standard window size within the design, irrespective of the make or type of under-floor engined chassis to be bodied. Once the body was fitted to the chassis, the mounting points on the crib rail were covered with a polished metal or aluminium alloy section. On completion of a full sized factory mock-up of the design, the company invited engineers from the large bus operating groups to inspect the new body. They were not

After the door unit was fitted the roof was lowered onto the shell. Assembly was completed when the rear end was mounted as in this factory scene.

After the floor and both sides had been mounted on the chassis, the front was fitted.

A fitter bolts a side frame to the rear end of a single deck vehicle.

Construction underway on a rear-end unit.

A door unit is fitted to a single deck vehicle. Only when this had been done could the roof be lowered onto the rest of the shell.

Craftsmen at work on a jig-held roof assembly.

The diagonally braced upper deck floor fitted to the first all aluminium body on the AEC Regent Mark III chassis, OKM 317.

in favour of the new design. Instead, concerns were raised over the use of folded panels. Operators believed these would be difficult to repair. Such reservations were held despite the fact that the company could have made parts available.

Ironically, this process reappeared 20 years later when the Leyland National body was launched. Interestingly, both bodies incorporated features which did not enter general use until the launch of the Leyland National single deck bus in 1972. The external appearance of the mock-up was similar to the contemporary Weymann single deck body. It featured a square front and a recessed, sloping driver's windscreen.

Using the experimental design, the company produced a new Saro lightweight single deck bus in 1952. It was mounted on the favoured Leyland Tiger Cub chassis and aluminium alloys were used throughout its construction. However, the new body also incorporated features of the old mock-up design. For example, the pillar sections were formed from the H-section alloy while the aluminium sheet was folded into a Z shape to form the roof sticks.

The Saro design consisted of eight main units: the two sides, front and rear ends, the front canopy, the roof, the floor and the entrance door unit. Unlike the previous Rivaloy body, except those destined for Auckland, the floor was built as a unit and fitted to the chassis as an assembly.

The internal luggage racks were manufactured in one piece. As a final operation, these were fitted into the body before positioning of the end unit. However, the crib

The mock-up of the lightweight, single deck body displaying the ribbed side panels and the crib rail cover strip.

The ribbed interior roof panel being assembled for the lightweight body mock-up.

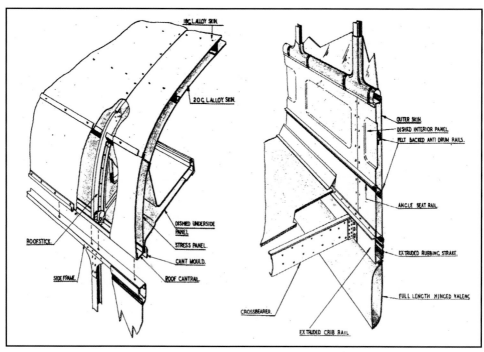

Saro roof body construction.   **Saro body side construction.**

rail section was also built into the body side and thus became the forerunner of the perimeter frame. This feature was introduced on the Volvo-Ailsa, Foden and Leyland Olympian double deck chassis 20 years later. In its standard form, the Saro single deck body weighed 1 ton 17 cwt and accommodated 44 seats.

Saro double deck bodies

The company produced its first double deck body in 1952 utilising many of the features incorporated within its single deck stablemate. The new body was mounted on a reconditioned AEC chassis and supplied to the Devon General Omnibus & Touring Company of Torquay.

Externally it was similar to the RT profile and became the lightest of all the double deck bodies produced by the company. It weighed 1 ton 19 cwt and was 5 cwt lighter than the first lightweight double deck body fitted to the AEC Regent Mark III chassis in 1951. Moreover, it was only 2 cwt heavier than the single deck body fitted to the Leyland Tiger Cub chassis.

The company produced a body suitable for mounting on the experimental rear engined Leyland Lowloader double deck chassis. Again, the design incorporated many of the parts used in the Saro single deck body. The design differed from its

The floor section of a Saro single deck body being lowered on to a Leyland Tiger Cub chassis. One of the completed body sides stands alongside ready to be lifted into place.

predecessors in that the main side pillars were extended from chassis level up to the top of the upper deck saloon windows. Previously, the lower deck framing was bolted to that of the the upper deck. In addition, the Leyland chassis was supplied with an aluminium alloy floor pan to which the main pillars were attached. As a result, the upper deck floor used a corrugated aluminium section similar to the chassis floor pan for lightness and strength.

In 1954, the final lightweight double deck bodies were built on AEC Regent Mark III chassis. These also incorporated the concept of main body side pillars extending from chassis level to the top of the upper deck windows. Although the rear of these two bodies retained the RT appearance, the design was modified to conform to the Crossley designed and built double deck bodies for Liverpool and formed the balance of their order for 100 buses.

All the Saro single and double deck bodies, plus most of the Rivaloy bodies used the Chobert riveting system. This was initially developed for use in the aircraft industry and the company used it to attach the external panels to the main body pillars. In order to fix two parts together, a hole was drilled through them into which a hollow stemmed rivet was fired. This eased assembly and made it easier to repair the body in later life should the need arise. Only one size of pop rivet was used in the building of the entire body.

One of the last two double deck bodies on AEC Regent Mark III chassis being built for Liverpool. The body side frames extend to the top of the upper deck windows.

The body for the prototype Leyland Lowloader during construction with its body side framing extending to the top of the upper deck window.

Staff in the production control department which was the nerve centre of the successful Saunders-Roe operation at Beaumaris.

Rivet holes in panels were produced by this multiple piercing machine, instead of by drilling, saving much production and assembly time.

Changing times

T he post-Second World War transition from aircraft modification to the production of bodywork for the passenger transport industry brought many changes for staff at the Beaumaris factory. However, as aluminium alloy was already used in the company's aircraft activities some of its machinery proved useful for this new work and in 1947 the company bought it from the Government.

Changing from one type of work to another within a short space of time was no mean feat. While the new production process was introduced, the factory's workforce completed a series of orders to refurbish public service vehicles. Vehicles began arriving at the factory in the early months of 1946 and the work continued until April 1947, when the last one was returned to its operator.

The factory's former aircraft hangers provided an ideal location for the refurbishment project. The vehicles were the only occupants of the hangers until the company started coachwork production while waiting for new chassis to arrive. The vast space in the hangers enabled it to use the flow line system of body assembly. For a time, echelon parking was used down one side to supplement the flow lines.

The hangers also housed the metal working machinery that was needed for the manufacture of vehicle bodywork. Often it was positioned to one side of the assembly lines or housed in buildings attached to the hangers. The assembly lines varied in number from two to four, depending on the volume of work in hand. The lines formed a U-shape allowing the chassis to enter from one end and turn before moving back down through the hanger.

When the jigs required for body unit the construction were installed in the hangers, the company reduced the space allocated to production resulting in the formation of body unit assembly lines. The contract for a large number of double deck bodies for London Transport resulted in the erection of further staging within the hangers. This provided access to the upper sections of the bodies.

The hangers also housed the paint booths used to apply the external finish to vehicle bodywork. This was accomplished with spray guns at a time when most manufacturers applied paint by hand using a brush. However, these facilities were

A lower deck side frame for an RT double deck body is constructed in a jig. A wooden block is fitted to the side window lower rail.

unable to deal with the large number of units passing through the hangers in 1949-1950. To overcome this Saunders employed outside contractors to paint some of the completed buses for the London Transport order.

The creation of the jig system enabled assembly workers to receive material in the form of kits. All the metal sections in the kits were cut to size and drilled, ready for assembly in the jigs. This reduced assembly time and also the need for employees to walk to and from the metal fabrication areas to collect material. The process also enabled payment to be made on piecework rates. The rates were derived from time and motion studies carried out during the various manufacturing and assembly processes.

The use of jigs and the flow line system enabled the company to produce large numbers of bus bodies without the need to increase production time and operational costs. The factory also employed both men and women on the bodywork production line at this time. During this era the hangers were not used for bodywork production. The factory still continued its interest in shipbuilding and the covered floor space was also utilised to manufacture other items including pontoons.

In 1953, the factory paint shop facilities were extended with the introduction of a new 13-bay paint shop. The first vehicles to pass through this were Saro single deck

Guy Arabs being built for Holland alongside a Foden. At this time the echelon method of parking was being utilised.

Buses from Southern Vectis and Northern General being refurbished in 1946.

Production lines for Northern General bodies mounted on AEC Regal Mark 1 chassis in 1946. On the left a line of United Automobile Bristol single deck vehicles is also undergoing refurbishment. A Southdown double deck stands in the background.

bodies for the BET Group order mounted on Leyland Tiger Cub chassis. A large store was established for materials and finished parts while a small fleet of vehicles including an articulated Leyland Comet lorry, was used to carry the PKD units.

Although the majority of bodywork constructed at the factory was complete, some of the bodies were delivered to the customer as shells. Normally, the PKD units and the shells were finished in grey primer, as were some complete bodies.

In order to attain a Ministry of Transport certificate of fitness for its vehicles, the company was required to tilt the first of a completed batch of bodies. This confirmed whether or not the completed vehicle satisfied legal requirements and was suitable for operation as a licensed passenger-carrying vehicle. Today a new vehicle is still issued with a similar certificate of initial fitness and this covers its working life subject to annual examination. In order to carry out the tilt test, a suitable platform was installed

This 1949 photograph shows the paint shop located in the main assembly hanger occupied by London Transport buses.

at Beaumaris. This was removed in 1950 and the tilt test facilities at Liverpool Corporation Passenger Transport's Edge Lane works were used instead. To pass the tilt test, the double deck bus was required to pass through an angle of 28 degrees from the vertical without the wheels leaving the platform while the upper deck was weighted to represent the maximum seated load. A single deck bus was required to tilt through a slightly greater angle of 35 degrees.

The production rates at Beaumaris varied. In one particularly busy month the company produced 20 double deck bodies for London Transport alongside single deck bodies for the Brazilian contract. Production or body numbers were issued although a complete record of allocations was not available at the time of writing. On the Saro single deck bodies supplied to the BET Group companies the bookmaker plates were used to house the numbers.

Upper deck frames for RT bodies under construction.

Saunders supplied bodies in partially knocked down (PKD) form. Here three kits can be seen mounted on left hand drive Leyland Royal Tiger chassis bound for Cuba.

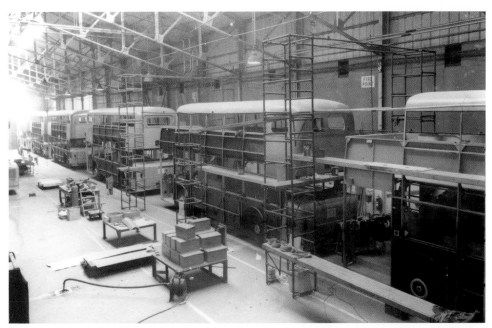

This photograph of the double deck body line taken in 1968 shows Leyland Atlantean buses for Devon General. Framing was erected in the hanger to allow ease of access.

Rivaloy bodies under construction for the Auckland Leyland Royal Tigers. The staging used in the construction of double deck bodies remained in place while this work was accomplished.

The tilt test. The first unpainted all aluminium double deck body mounted on an AEC Regent Mark III chassis undergoes testing at Liverpool Corporation's Edge Lane works. A Liverpool tram is visible in the background.

In 1968, Cammell-Laird restarted production of double deck bodywork at Beaumaris. A new production line was established including the use of staging. However, production levels failed to match that of the London Transport contract. Once the MCW work was completed, the staging was removed and the floor space used for other production.

The first double deck body for Southdown undergoing a tilt test at Beaumaris.

Spreading the word

As with most companies and their products, publicity played an enormously important part in ensuring that the fortunes of the Saunders company were successful, particularly with regard to its bus building endeavours. Newspaper and magazine articles, advertising in the trade press, exhibition and even bodywork motifs all played a vital part in brand awareness and spreading the message of what the company could offer its customers.

Advertising

During the company's years of involvement with bodywork production, a number of eye-catching advertisements appeared within the trade and technical press. Many of these used news of orders that had been placed with the company for the supply of bodywork to reinforce the message that the Saunders product was generating interest worldwide and worthy of attention. Sometimes advertisements also relied on details of recent prestigious deliveries to spread the message.

The company also used the important medium of advertising to announce the release of new body styles and designs. On these occasions pamphlets were also used to raise the company's profile and promote the latest product. Photographic material figured largely in all of these methods. In addition to direct advertising the company also circulated reprints of technical press articles among bus and coach operators, both at home and abroad. Many of these descriptive articles were later used within tender documents to support the detail of quotations.

Bodywork motifs

Like most similar companies, Saunders was proud of the products it turned out. In keeping with the practice of the day the company was keen to stamp its mark on the bodies that left its Beaumaris factory. Initially it used the acronym SEAS on the bodies fitted to vertical front-engined chassis. The letters were formed within an oval shape and cast into the clutch housing covers at the bottom of the front bulkhead in

A Saunders-Roe advertisement which appeared in the Leyland Journal, September 1953 showing an illustration of the Saro body on a Leyland Tiger Cub chassis.

An advertisement used by Saunders-Roe in 1950. From the top, it features Rivaloy bodies in a number of guises:

1 On a front-engined chassis as used by Crosville and Lincolnshire.

2 On a Commer chassis.

3 On a front-engined double deck chassis as supplied to Maidstone & District.

4 On a front-engined single deck chassis proposed for Maidstone & District.

5 On an under-floor single deck chassis as supplied for export.

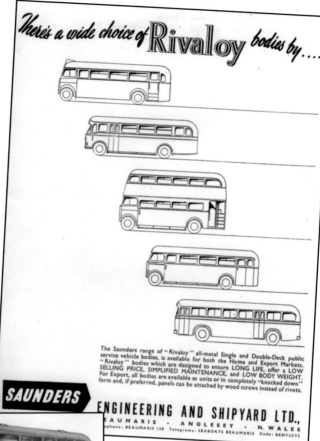

There's a wide choice of **Rivaloy** bodies by....

The Saunders range of "Rivaloy" all-metal Single and Double-Deck public service vehicle bodies, is available for both the Home and Export Markets. "Rivaloy" bodies which are designed to ensure LONG LIFE, offer a LOW SELLING PRICE, SIMPLIFIED MAINTENANCE, and LOW BODY WEIGHT. For Export, all bodies are available as units or in completely "knocked down" form and, if preferred, panels can be attached by wood screws instead of rivets.

SAUNDERS ENGINEERING AND SHIPYARD LTD.,
BEAUMARIS · ANGLESEY · N. WALES
Telephone: BEAUMARIS 130 Telegrams: SEABOATS BEAUMARIS Code: BENTLEYS

AT HOME *or* **ABROAD**

Since the first deliveries of "Rivaloy" all-metal bodies, early in 1950, their many attractive features including a low selling price, have established for them a wide demand in the Home and Export markets. One of the latest orders is for Compania Uruguaya de Transportes Colectivos S.A. of Uruguay, who have ordered 25 Leyland "Royal Tiger" chassis fitted with "Rivaloy" all-metal bodies.

SAUNDERS ROE (ANGLESEY) LTD
COACH DIVISION
BEAUMARIS ANGLESEY NORTH WALES
Telephone: Beaumaris 130
Telegrams: Searoads, Beaumaris
Code: Bentleys

DESIGNERS AND BUILDERS OF
OMNIBUS BODIES AND LIGHT ALLOY CRAFT

A Saunders-Roe advertisement featuring the Rivaloy all aluminium bodies that was published in The Leyland Journal's, May 1951 edition.

the lower saloon. Although later versions retained the same oval shape the inscription was modified to read Coachwork by SEAS Beaumaris.

The advent of the under-floor engined and vertical front-engined chassis eliminated the need for a cast clutch housing as part of the bulkhead, so the company produced a diamond-shaped transfer for display within a body's saloon. A blue border was used to accommodate the yellow lettered inscription: SEAS Coachwork, SEA Ltd, Beaumaris, Anglesey, North Wales. Inside the border, the transfer featured a view of the Menai Bridge and on it a double deck bus.

In 1951, a new motif was introduced following a change in the company's name. The design appeared in all of the company's literature and formed in pressed aluminium on vehicle bodywork. The new logo contained a square, centred within a distinctive winged design. On top of this was a further rectangle containing the letters SARO above the words Saunders Roe (Anglesey) Ltd. Underneath, the date 1830 featured as a reminder of the original company's founding year.

In many respects, the new motif was adapted from an existing company logo. The company's aircraft division was already using the winged design and had also used the Saro abbreviation since the formation of Saunders-Roe in 1928. Alongside its traditional use, the company also used the new motif to carry information on vehicles supplied against the BET group's order for 500 Leyland Tiger Cub chassis in 1952. Each motif carried the vehicle's body number and month and year of manufacture.

Exhibitions

During the 1940s and 50s, the company exhibited bus bodywork in the biennial commercial motor shows held at the Earl's Court Exhibition Centre, London. At the early shows, the company decided to display completed vehicles on chassis manufacturer's stands while some, including the first completed vehicle in 1948, were shown in the demonstration park outside the exhibition hall.

In 1952, the company decided to break with tradition and had its own stand inside the exhibition hall. The Saunders-Roe (Anglesey) Ltd display featured the new double deck body built for Birmingham City Transport and the Saro single deck body

The Saunders-Roe bodywork insignia.

Illustration shows 'Saro' light weight body on Leyland 'Tiger Cub' Chassis

A pamphlet extolling the virtues of the Saro light weight body on a Leyland Tiger Cub chassis that was produced by Saunders-Roe.

The Saunders-Roe stand at the 1952 Earl's Court, London, Commercial Motor Show. On display are a Saro-bodied Leyland Tiger Cub for Ribble and a Guy Arab for Birmingham City Transport. The strange looking sectioned Saro body assembly is visible on the right.

The Leyland stand at the 1950 Commercial Motor Show featuring a Leyland Tiger bound for Cuba. This is believed to be one of four demonstrators altered to production vehicle standard. In addition, the Leyland bodied Royal Tiger and Leicester Corporation Leyland Titan double deck bus can be seen at the back of the stand.

produced for Ribble Motor Services. The stand also displayed a sectioned part-body used to illustrate the constructional features of the new Saro body. After the show, the sectional body was taken back to the Beaumaris factory and ended its days as an office for the supervisor in the apprentice training school.

In 1954 the company proudly showed off the prototype Leyland Lowloader rear-engined double deck bus in the show's demonstration park. Sadly, this occasion marked the last appearance of a Saunders-Roe bodied vehicle at the show.

Within two years, the company had received its last order, the Auckland contract, bringing to a close a glorious era in the company's manufacture of bodywork for public service vehicle operators.

Beaumaris bodies

Vehicle bodies produced at Beaumaris were despatched far and wide. Many saw long service at home and abroad for vastly different operators. What follows is an inventory of all known vehicle bodies produced at Beaumaris during the period 1946 to 1956 for use as public service vehicles in both the UK and abroad. The schedule also includes Metro Cammell Weymann designed bodies manufactured at the factory and the Superior coachwork kits assembled on behalf of MCW in 1968 and 1969. In addition, details are provided for those bodies refurbished during 1946 and 1947 before production of new bodywork began.

In many cases, production of bodywork for larger orders stretched over a number of years. Therefore, the year in which production was started is included in the list. Importantly, bodywork details are also shown in the years of production but this information is not presented in the order of manufacture or the sequence in which they were delivered from the factory. This is because it was not possible to track down the company's production schedules. Finally, the company also received orders for bodywork that, for one reason or another, was never built.

Refurbished bodywork

During 1946 and the early months of 1947, Saunders launched its involvement in bus building by refurbishing the following known vehicles at its Beaumaris factory.

Southern Vectis Omnibus Co.

Fleet no.	Reg. no.	Vehicle	Bodywork
11	DL 9719	Dennis Lancet	Duple C32F
14	ADL 629	Dennis Lancet	Harrington C32F
16	ADL 400	Dennis Lancet	Margham C32F
19	GN 1379	AEC Regal	Harrington C32F

Harrington-bodied Dennis Lancet ADL 629 from the Southern Vectis fleet, which was refurbished at Beaumaris.

Northern General Transport

This Brush-bodied Leyland Tiger TS8, registration number CU 3947 and fleet number 867 in the Northern General fleet was also refurbished at Beaumaris.

Fleet no.	Reg. no.	Vehicle	Bodywork
867	CU 3947	Leyland Tiger TS8	Brush C30F
874	CU 3954	Leyland Tiger TS8	Duple C30F

Southdown Motor Services

Fleet no.	Reg. no.	Vehicle	Bodywork
104	BUF 204	Leyland TD4	Short L26/26R
1419	BUF 999	Leyland Tiger TS7	Harrington B32R

United Automobile Services

Fleet no.	Reg. no.	Vehicle	Bodywork
BJO 54	BHN 249	Bristol JO5G	ECW
BJO 70	CHN 270	Bristol JO5G	ECW
BJO 100	CHN 300	Bristol JO5G	ECW
BJO 106	CHN 306	Bristol JO5G	ECW

New bodywork

1946

Northern General Transport

The first production run of new bodywork at the Beaumaris factory resulted in the manufacture of 18 single deck bodies to the BET design for the Northern General Transport Company. Externally, the side panels were flared at the bottom and a two-bar chrome plated quarter bumper was fitted to each of the rear corner panels. The front entrance was of a porch-type design with double folding entrance doors. An emergency door was also centrally fitted at the rear. The panel beneath the driver's windscreen was curved and the bodies seated 36 passengers. They were finished in the lined red and cream livery of Northern General. Delivery took place in November and December 1946.

After two or three years in service, Northern General complained of excessive movement in the bodyframe and all 18 buses were returned to Beaumaris. Work to rectify the problem was carried out in two stages between 1949 and 1951. It included

Fleet no.	Reg. no.	Vehicle	Bodywork
1117-1134	CN 9957-9974	AEC Regal Mark 1	B36F

The interior of a Northern General single deck bus.

the strengthening of the entrance door pillar, the front and rear domes, the rear emergency door framing and the driver's cab pillar. The newly strengthened entrance door pillar resulted in the repositioning of an opening window in the body side.

At chassis frame level, additional cross bracing was also fitted between the waist rail frame and the body pillars. This method was similar to bracing introduced on later bodywork.

A rear view of a BET Federation style body on an AEC Regal Mark 1 chassis for Northern General, fleet number 1119, registration number CN 9959.

A completed AEC Regal Mark 1 with a BET-style body ready for delivery to Northern General, registration number CN 9959.

Foden

To improve the delivery of new vehicles to operators, the Foden company placed an order for the production of 24 single deck bodies. Mounted on Foden PVSC5 chassis, these were built to a Saunders' design.

They had plain side panels and a front entrance complete with a sliding door. The emergency exit was positioned opposite the entrance door, immediately behind the driver's cab. The rear wings were flared at the base and the raised bottom of the lower panels was continued around the rear of the body to form a bumper section.

A canopy was built over the engine to include fitting of a single line destination display. Polished aluminium mouldings were also fitted to the waistline of the body. In some cases, the area within these mouldings was painted in a contrasting colour to suit the operator's livery. Finally, the bottom of the driver's windscreen was curved to match the contour of the full width front of the Foden chassis. Originally, Saunders agreed to body a number of double deck chassis for Foden. However, such plans were not realised and therefore, the company only built and fitted single deck bodies onto the Foden chassis. The vehicles that were constructed to fulfill the Foden contract were delivered direct to the following operators:

W. Kirkpatrick, Marple, Stockport

Fleet no.	Reg. no.	Vehicle	Bodywork
—	JMA 30	Foden PVSC5	B37F

Green Bus Services, Rugeley

Fleet no.	Reg. no.	Vehicle	Bodywork
16-19/21	MRF 635-8/40	Foden PVSC5	B37F

1947
Green Bus Services, Rugeley

Fleet no.	Reg. no.	Vehicle	Bodywork
20	MRF 639	Foden PVSC5	B37F

Crown Coaches, Birtley

Fleet no.	Reg. no.	Vehicle	Bodywork
49-53	GUP 451-455	Foden PVSC5	B37F
57-60	CNL 451-454	Foden PVSC5	B37F
62-64	CNL 893-895	Foden PVSC5	B35F

NB: CNL 893 was supplied to Alexander of Falkirk as fleet number F1 and registered as AWG 586. However, it was re-allocated to Crown Coaches. Another chassis was supplied to Alexander which then assumed the original fleet and registration numbers.

One of the Foden chassis bodied by Saunders and supplied to the Green Bus Services.
This vehicle carried the registration number MRF 636.

Salopia Saloon Coaches
Whitchurch, Salop

Fleet no.	Reg. no.	Vehicle	Bodywork
51	DUX 789	Foden PVSC5	B35F

Caerphilly Urban District Council

Fleet no.	Reg. no.	Vehicle	Bodywork
10-11	GTX 310-311	Foden PVSC5	B36F (Rebuilt 1956)
12-13	GTX 762-763	Foden PVSC5	B36F

Beech of Hanley

Beech of Hanley, a Guy agent, ordered 15 single deck bodies. These were fitted onto Guy Arab Mark III chassis and were almost identical to those built on the Foden chassis. However, their external appearance was different and included the use of a straight, rather than curved, lower rail on the driver's windscreen. Production of the Beech bodies followed the Foden order and the first were completed early in 1947.

Aluminium mouldings were fitted at waist rail level on each side of the body. These mouldings started at the front of the vehicle and swept down to the rear wing. Again, depending on the colour scheme chosen by the operator, the area between these mouldings could be painted in a contrasting colour, thus forming a flash effect on the body sides.

Despite the extreme shortage of new vehicles at the time, operators still endeavoured to place orders for new vehicles in the hope of meeting at least some of their needs. This practice resulted in chassis orders being transferred from one operator to another or even cancelled. These changes are apparent in the chassis listed below. The recipients of the completed vehicles are also shown and where relevant, the chassis allocation made by Guy Motors at the time the order was placed is included.

Ripponden & District

Fleet no.	Reg. no.	Vehicle	Bodywork
11	FWX 330	Guy Arab III	B37F

Worth's Services, Enstone

Fleet no.	Reg. no.	Vehicle	Bodywork
—	CBW 600	Guy Arab III	B37F

Berresford Motors Cheddleton

Fleet no.	Reg. no.	Vehicle	Bodywork
15	MRF 528	Guy Arab III	B37F
16	MRF 530	Guy Arab III	B37F

NB: Guy Motors allocated the fleet number 15 chassis to Milton Bus Services and fleet number 16 chassis to Green Bus Services.

One of the Guy Arab Mark III chassis bodied by Saunders and supplied to Berresford, registration number MRF 528.

Brown Bros. Sapcote, Leicester

Fleet no.	Reg. no.	Vehicle	Bodywork
—	DUT 570	Guy Arab III	B37F

NB: Guy allocated this vehicle's chassis to Green Bus Services.

J Vessey, Hibaldstow, Brigg, Lincolnshire

Fleet no.	Reg. no.	Vehicle	Bodywork
—	DFW 169	Guy Arab III	B37F
—	DFW 170	Guy Arab III	B37F

NB: Guy allocated the first chassis to W Earth of Boston and the second to the South Notts Bus Co. who later operated the vehicle.

Mainwaring Bros. Stoke-on-Trent

Fleet no.	Reg. no.	Vehicle	Bodywork
—	MRF 520	Guy Arab III	B37F
—	MRF 531	Guy Arab III	B37F

NB: Guy allocated the former chassis to Crick, Upper Benefield
and the latter to Green Bus Services.

Hudson's Bus Co. Horncastle, Lincs

Fleet no.	Reg. no.	Vehicle	Bodywork
18	DFW 550	Guy Arab III	B37F
19	DFW 551	Guy Arab III	B37F

NB: Guy allocated the former chassis to Vessey, Hibaldstow. It was later
fitted with a Duple C35F body. The latter chassis went to Graves, Nottingham and
was fitted with a Plaxton C35F body.

A rear view of a Guy Arab built for Hudsons of Horncastle, showing how the flared
rear wings were continued across the back of the body.

One of the single deck bodies supplied on Guy Arab III chassis to Thomas Beckett,
registration number KVT 348.

Thomas Beckett, Bucknall

Fleet no.	Reg. no.	Vehicle	Bodywork
—	KVT 348	Guy Arab III	B37F

NB: Guy allocated this vehicle's chassis to Milton Bus Services.

Milton Bus Services, Milton

Fleet no.	Reg. no.	Vehicle	Bodywork
—	MRF 348	Guy Arab III	B37F
—	MRF 349	Guy Arab III	B37F
—	MRF 350	Guy Arab III	B37F

NB: Guy Motors allocated this MRF 348 chassis to Crick, Upper Benefield and
the others to Beech, Hanley as dealer stock.

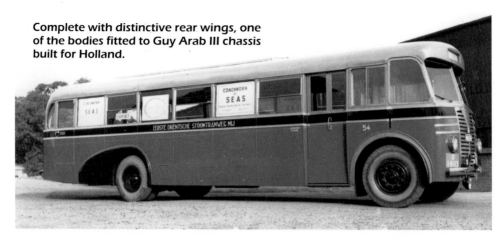

Complete with distinctive rear wings, one of the bodies fitted to Guy Arab III chassis built for Holland.

De Nederlandsle Motoren Maatschappij NV, Rotterdam

The Guy Agent in Holland ordered 60 single deck bodies. These were the first to be exported by Saunders-Roe and formed part of an order for 120 vehicles for use by various operators in Holland.

The bodies were mounted on long wheelbase Guy Arab Mark III left hand drive chassis and seated 45 passengers. Continental in appearance, they sported a full width front covering the Guy radiator and were fitted with double folding entrance doors. Each body had an entrance behind the front wheels and an emergency exit at the rear of the body on the same side as the entrance. Internally, a seat for three passengers was fitted across the front bulkhead and an emergency escape hatch was installed in the roof.

In February 1947, the first chassis arrived at the factory and the first vehicle was completed in June of that year. Once the last chassis had arrived in September 1947, the company was able to complete the production of the bodies by the end of the year.

An interior view of one of the single deck bodies fitted to Guy and Foden chassis.

Finished in the colour schemes of the intended operators, Saunders-Roe used the polished aluminium waist rail mouldings and the distinctively designed rear wings to provide an area for a second colour within the paint scheme.

During their transportation, one of the vehicles was

damaged and its body was replaced before delivery to Holland. However, after a period of service there, Dutch coachbuilders were given the task of providing new bodywork for many of the Saunders-Roe supplied vehicles.

Southdown Motor Services

The first double deck bodies to be built at Beaumaris were for a batch of nine vehicles for Southdown and fitted to reconditioned Leyland Titan double deck chassis.

The bodywork incorporated many features specified by the operator including a visor over the windscreen and the use of a small window under the stairs, on the driver's side of the body. Internally, saloon heaters were also fitted and both the lower and upper saloons were finished to the high standard requirements of the company.

The first vehicle was completed in May 1947 with the balance of the order being delivered in June and July of the same year.

The first double deck body that Saunders supplied to Southdown, mounted on a reconditioned Leyland Titan chassis.

Fleet no.	Reg. no.	Vehicle	Bodywork
960	AUF 660	Leyland Titan TD3C	H28/26R
961	AUF 661	Leyland Titan TD3C	H28/26R
960	BUF 215	Leyland Titan TD4	H28/26R
115	BUF 217	Leyland Titan TD4	H28/26R
117	BUF 228	Leyland Titan TD4	H28/26R
128	BUF 235	Leyland Titan TD4	H28/26R
135	EUF 183	Leyland Titan TD5	H28/26R
183	EUF 186	Leyland Titan TD5	H28/26R
186	EUF 199	Leyland Titan TD5	H28/26R

An interior view of the lower deck format of the bodies supplied to Southdown.
A Clayton saloon heater was fitted on the front bulkhead and the window finishers
were of polished wood.

Midland General Omnibus Co.

Twenty five single deck bodies were supplied to Midland General on Leyland Tiger PS1 chassis to the exact specifications of this Balfour Beatty Group Company.

Externally they were similar to the Weymann-built BET specification bodies previously supplied to Midland General. Plain side panels were used between the front and rear axles. However, the panels behind the rear axle and rear panels were flared. A chrome strip was also fitted to the bottom of these, starting at the back of the rear wings, on either side of the body. In addition, the design of the rear wings was similar to those fitted to the bodies built on Guy and Foden chassis.

The emergency door was fitted behind the driver's cab and a locker was installed in the rear of the body. A detachable destination board was fitted on each side, while destination blinds and route number displays were positioned at the front and back. Thirteen of the bodies were supplied as 35-seat buses. The remainder were fitted with semi-coach style seats incorporating armrests. These accommodated just 32 passengers. The completed vehicles were all delivered by December 1947.

A Leyland Tiger PS1 chassis bodied for The Midland General company.

Fleet no.	Reg. no.	Vehicle	Bodywork
200-224	DFW 551	KRB 86-110	B35F/DP32F

NB: numbers: 200/3-5/8/11-12/15-16/20-21/23-24 were supplied as B35F
numbers 201-2/6-7/9/10/13-14/17-19/22 as DP32F

A rear view of Midland General fleet number 206. The rear locker doors and the detachable side destination board are clearly visible. The rear of this body resembles the Weymann single deck body of the period.

An interior view of one of the single deck bodies supplied on Leyland chassis to Midland General. Like the others, fleet number 206 boasted polished wood finishers and the Clayton saloon heater.

Durban Motor Transport

The 20 double deck bodies ordered by South African operator Durban Moor Transport were the first to be built and supplied for export by Saunders-Roe. More significantly, these were the only double deck bodies to be exported by the company.

Mounted on right-hand drive AEC Regent Mark III chassis, these 8ft wide, 30ft long bodies were similar to those supplied to Southdown. However, the lower and upper deck side windows were covered by two external rails and a trough was fitted at the bottom of the rear panels. Racks were also positioned below the rear upper deck emergency door to accommodate passengers' fishing rods. A tip-up seat was provided on the rear platform for the conductor's use.

The bodies were finished in a livery of ivory and grey. In addition, a darker grey was used on the wings, lining and lifeguards. Chrome plated bumpers were fitted to the front and rear of the completed vehicles. Semaphore direction indicators were installed on each side of the body and a direction arrow was fitted in the lower rear panel at waist rail level. Internally, the upper saloon roof was double skinned. The bodies seated 26 people in the lower saloon and 32 people above. The order was completed in May 1948 and all the vehicles were shipped out as deck cargo from Birkenhead docks.

A view of the lower deck interior of the double deck body supplied to Durban. Extensive use was made of polished wood finishers.

One of the eight-foot wide, double deck bodies supplied to Durban. The racks on the back were for the passengers' fishing rods.

A forward looking view of the upper deck interior of the bodies supplied to Durban on AEC Regent chassis. The roof was double skinned.

Lisbon Electric Tramways

In September 1946, an announcement was made in the AEC Gazette that Lisbon Electric Tramways had placed an order with the company for the supply of 60 AEC Regal Mark III left hand drive chassis. Of these vehicles 50 would be fitted with single deck bodies produced by Saunders. The remaining vehicles were to receive bodies supplied by Weymann, of which 10 were to be supplied as shells for completion by the operator in Lisbon.

However, the company's actual order was for 62 chassis. Weymann were asked to supply 12 bodies in shell form. At the time of this announcement, one of a batch of six AEC Regal Mark 1 single deck chassis recently completed by Weymann, was sent to Beaumaris for inspection. This provided an ideal opportunity for the Saunders design staff to examine the vehicle, prior to its shipment to Lisbon. Although this body was mounted on a right-hand drive chassis, the design provided an indication of the requirements to be met for the construction of the new bodies.

The first chassis was delivered to the factory in January 1947. The remainder followed between June that year and April 1948. Under this contract, the total number of vehicles supplied to Lisbon was increased by a further two orders resulting in a total of 102, of which 60 bodies were supplied by Saunders. In an effort to speed up the delivery of buses to Lisbon, Saunders was approached to supply bodies as shells. The first 10 sent to Lisbon are thought to have been in this form. Once completed by the operator, the vehicles then entered service in March 1948.

Lisbon Tramways was responsible for setting out the specification of the bodies. They were eight feet wide and accommodated seating for 24 people. At the rear of the body, provision was made for 12 standing passengers with a further standing space for nine at the

An article from the AEC Gazette of September 1946.

EXPORT

A.E.C. SECURES BIG LISBON TRAMWAYS' CONTRACT

More Passenger and Goods Chassis For Denmark

A considerable increase in the population of Lisbon, particularly during the war years, has thrown an ever-growing strain upon the transport services of Portugal's capital city. In 1944, for instance (the last year for which figures are available) the number of passengers carried on the Lisbon Electric tramway's system exceeded 200,000,000, representing an increase of 14,000,000 over the previous year, and 80,000,000 over the last pre-war year.

Consequently the Company is now, at the first favourable opportunity, embarking upon a comprehensive long-term plan of improvements estimated (in 1945) to cost upwards of £1,000,000.

One of the first actions to be taken with the aim of supplementing existing services has been to order a fleet of new machines, and, in this connection, A.E.C. is able to announce this month the award of a contract from the LISBON ELECTRIC TRAMWAYS, LTD., for SIXTY-TWO, Mark III SERIES, SINGLE-DECKERS FITTED WITH LEFT-HAND STEERING.

Fifty of these machines will be shipped complete with all-metal bodies, specially constructed for conditions in the Portuguese capital, by Saunders Engineering & Shipyard, Ltd.

Lisbon Electric Tramways, Ltd., have been operating A.E.C.'s since 1940 when the first six single-deckers went into operation. There is no doubt that the high standard of service given by these machines, particularly under the exceptionally onerous conditions of the last six years, have greatly influenced the placing of this most important contract, and also that for six single-deckers which preceded it last year.

In the last issue there was announced an order from the same undertaking for three A.E.C. "Monarch" vehicles to be used for permanent way and other work.

From NORDISK DIESELAUTO, A.E.C.'s distributors in Denmark, has come a new contract covering the supply of a further 20 "Regal" Mark III single-deck chassis and 16 "Matador" goods chassis. A number of the latter will be used by Danish operators for long-distance hauls extending considerably beyond the borders of that country.

The inclusion of new single-deckers in a Norwegian fleet where there have been Southall-built machines for ten years will follow the placing of a contract with A.E.C. by SCHOYENS BICENTRALER, Oslo, for six "Regals." A.E.C.'s

115

95

A completed SEAS body on an AEC Regal Mark III chassis awaits delivery to Lisbon. The front bumper has yet to be fitted to fleet number 66.

front of the bus. The body also had a rear entrance and front exit. A destination and numeral display was located in the front canopy while a similar display was fitted into the roof cove panel adjacent to the rear entrance. Ventilated louvres were placed on each side of the body over the side saloon windows.

Internally, the side windows were provided with pull down sun blinds. Slots were also made in the pillars, located on each side of the window. Sliding doors were fitted in the front and rear, entrance and exit.

In addition, semaphore direction indicators were placed on each side of the body and a chrome bumper fitted across the front of the bus. However, the Saunders-built bodies differed from those of Weymann. They sported a square front profile and a

The interior of a single deck body supplied to Lisbon. The standing area is portioned off on the left-hand side while pull cord signal bell cords run down either side of the body above the windows. Slots are provided in the window finishers for the pull down blinds.

96

This Weymann-bodied AEC Regal Mark I was photographed during a visit to Beaumaris. Built in 1946 it was one of six similar buses to enter service in Lisbon in 1947. It carried the fleet Number 11 and chassis number 06624006.

straight bottom was given to the driver's windscreen. In contrast, the Weymann body featured a smooth frontal, curved design.

Buenos Aires Transport Board

The third major export order placed with Saunders consisted of 50 single deck bodies. Mounted on eight-foot wide, left hand drive ACLO (AEC) Regal Mark III chassis, these dual-doored bodies were much influenced by Latin American tastes.

Following extensive research into the design preferences of South American operators, Saunders created a new single deck design. The full frontal bodies included the use of narrow window bays and flat sides. At the rear of the body, a large bottom-hinged emergency door was incorporated into the window. The AEC radiator remained exposed and the front wings extended down to the bottom of it. Polished aluminium mouldings were positioned at waist rail level along the body sides and the enclosed area was used to display a colour contrast to the main body shade. A chromed steel bumper was also fitted across the front and back.

The painting styles used on the bodies varied. Some were supplied with a wine coloured waistband while others had similarly coloured front wings to contrast with the aluminium-coloured body. Full drop windows were also fitted in each of the main window bays and straps were positioned in the saloon roof for standing passengers. Internally, the side windows had adjustable pull down sun blinds and the entrance

Possibly the first bus to be supplied as part of the Argentinian contract awaits delivery. The extension of the front wings is covered by the chromium plated bumper fitted across the front of the vehicle.

and exit were fitted with double folding doors. The bodies seated 35 with capacity for 23 standing passengers. In January 1948, the first vehicle was completed and sent to London for inspection by the Argentine Ambassador. Once approved, the vehicles marked the first complete set of buses to be exported from this country to South

Featuring the name of its new owner on the side together with a fleet number this is one of the buses exported to Argentina.

America since the end of the Second World War. After delivery, all the buses were handed over to the Argentine government for use on a new service between Buenos Aires and Lujan. Starting in November 1948, the buses were operated under a company known as Empress Nacional 17 De Octubre.

Northern General Transport

One single deck body was supplied to Northern General Transport Co. Ltd on a re-conditioned Leyland chassis. This was similar to those supplied the previous year on AEC Regal chassis. The side panels between the front and rear axles were plain on this body and the rear wings similar to those fitted to the bodies mounted on Guy and Foden chassis. The bus was finished in the operator's standard livery of red and cream with lined panels. The vehicle was returned to the company on March 1, 1948.

Fleet no.	Reg. no.	Vehicle	Bodywork
786	APT 785	Leyland Tiger TS7	B36F

This single deck body was supplied to Northern General on a reconditioned Leyland Tiger chassis. The photograph was taken at the company's central works at Bensham after the vehicle had entered service. Some of its window louvres are missing.

1948

Maidstone & District Motor Services

The third batch of double deck bodies built at Beaumaris consisted of a 40-strong order for Maidstone & District Motor Services. Mounted on Bristol K6A chassis, they were of a similar design to those supplied to both Southdown and Durban.

The lower body panels were flared at the bottom and a chrome strip was fitted around the rear of the body. Semaphore direction indicators were positioned on each side of the body while a permanent ventilator was fitted in the front upper deck dome. Ventilators were also placed in three of the lower saloon window bays and four upper deck window bays. Finally, mirrors were fitted in the lower saloon bulkhead.

The completed buses weighed 7 ton 10 cwt 1 qr and the first vehicles were delivered in May 1948 and the last one in September of that year. These double deck bodies were to be the last built to the pre-war Short Bros. design.

Fleet no.	Reg. no.	Vehicle	Bodywork
DH 204-243	JKM 901-940	Bristol K6A	H30/26R

This lower deck had mirrors fitted to the bulkhead and polished wood window surrounds. The clutch cover displays very prominently the SEAS acronym.

Awaiting delivery to
Maidstone & District, this
double deck body was
mounted on a
Bristol K6A chassis.

The upper deck of a
Maidstone & District double
deck body. The single skin
roof is clearly shown.

This photograph shows the entrance and exits fitted in the body of a bus that was part of the Sao Palo contract. The vehicle is complete with the operator's name and associated lettering as well as a very prominent fleet number.

Some of the ACLO Regal III buses bound for Sao Paulo, Brazil, are loaded aboard ship at London Docks.

Companhia de Transportes Colectivos, Sao Paulo, Brazil

In November 1947, AEC announced an order for Brazil for vehicles worth around £500,000. The 91 Saunders-Roe bodies supplied as part of that were mounted on left-hand drive ACLO (AEC) Regal Mark III long wheelbase chassis and were similar to those supplied the previous year to Argentina.

Experimental work was carried out in the factory in an attempt to develop a new, full width, front design. This covered the AEC radiator and the previously used chromed steel bumper was replaced with a substantial channel section mounted across the front of the bus. Direction indicator lamps were fitted in the front and rear body panels,

This rear view shows the arrangement of the emergency exit rear window.

while marker lights were positioned in the front and rear domes. The emergency door was also fitted in the rear window and again hinged at the bottom. All the bodies had seats for 37 passengers and roof straps for a further 23.

Decorative polished mouldings were placed along the sides of the body and across the rear panels. However, one body was completed in a different livery style to the remainder and featured front window pillars shaped to match the profile of the rear dome. A V-shape was painted on the front panel in a contrasting colour which was carried down the body sides. A similarly coloured panel, carrying the operator's title, was also painted on the cove panels on each side.

The main production batch vehicles were painted in a dual coloured livery with polished mouldings fitted to the body waist rail. Interestingly, the first production body differed in that it used a separate route number and destination display.

Following the completion of the first vehicle in September 1948, the company estimated it could complete 25 vehicles each month. In October, the Brazilian Minister inspected the first bus in London and once approved, it was moved to a display in the demonstration park of Earl's Court. There it took pride of place among the other exhibits in the first Commercial Motor Show held following the end of the Second World War. The company completed the last vehicle of this contract in September 1949.

Looking towards the driver's cab of one of the vehicles supplied to Brazil. The polished wood window surrounds and window pan slots for the pull down sun blinds, fixed over each window can be clearly seen. A pull cord bell course runs the length of the saloon on both side above the windows. Roof mounted rails are provided for standing passengers. The clutch cover reads Coachwork by SEAS Beaumaris. The interiors of the bodies closely resembled those supplied on similar chassis to Argentina.

The 'odd' body supplied under the Sao Paulo contract with its rounded windows and modified livery.

London Transport

In December 1946, London Transport advertised in the trade press for coachbuilders to submit tenders for the supply of bodies on their AEC Regent RT chassis. They wanted to speed up delivery of its new buses and subsequently received its first approach from Saunders. An initial order was placed for 240 double deck bodies, but in January 1947, London Transport increased this to 250.

Originally, the company intended to build the bodies to a Saunders design, modified to accept the London RT chassis. It intended to supply 100 of these between January and April 1948, with the completion of the order by December of that year. However, after the order had been placed, a newly completed Weymann-bodied RT was sent to the factory in August 1947. When the vehicle, RT 410, was inspected by the Saunders design staff the management at Beaumaris decided to redesign the Saunders double deck body. The new version was intended to conform as near as possible to the London design, while using the Saunders frame material. As a result of these changes, the production of the double deck bodies was delayed. In addition, export work remained the main concern on the company's production line and the required jigs were not installed until April, 1948.

In November 1948, the first London bus was completed and the following month it was delivered to London Transport as RT 1152. Following representations by the Saunders management to London Transport in December 1948, a further 50 bodies

Fleet no.	Reg. no.	Vehicle	Bodywork
RT 1152-1181	JXC 460-489	AEC Regent RT	H30/26R
RT 1182-1251	KGK 651-720	AEC Regent RT	H30/26R
RT 1252-1351	KLB 501-600	AEC Regent RT	H30/26R
RT 1352-1401	KXW 451-500	AEC Regent RT	H30/26R
RT 4218-4267	KYY 821-870	AEC Regent RT	H30/26R

were ordered increasing the total number to 300. In July 1949, production levels rose to a maximum of 20 bodies a month although this figure varied in relation to the supply of AEC chassis. The last body, numbered RT 4267, was completed in January 1951 and a month later delivered to London Transport.

The completed Saunders body was similar to those produced by both Weymann and Park Royal. However, the Saunders body design shared Metro Cammell Weymann's distinction of using the respective maker's standard frame materials. Importantly, the Saunders bodies were also the last vehicles to be supplied to London Transport in the

The Weymann-bodied London Transport RT 410 being examined by drawing office and works staff at Beaumaris.

Newly completed RT 11458 awaits delivery from Beaumaris to London Transport. The vehicle's front advertisements were fitted at the factory.

A view of the upper saloon of a London RT double deck body built at Beaumaris.

The lower saloon of a London RT body looking towards the driver's cab.

early post-war livery. Featuring cream upper deck window surrounds, each body sported a front route number box housed in the roof dome.

In 1994 one Saunders bodied RT, owned by Ensign Bus, RT 3062 registered as KXW 171 remained in service although the body was transferred from its original chassis. At this time other Saunders bodies mounted on the chassis of RT 742 and 3132 were still in use at the University of California, owned by the Unitran company. Other examples have also been preserved.

1949

Crosville Motor Services

While the work of redesigning the double deck body was being carried out, Saunders turned its attention to designing a new single deck body. Its first batch of these bodies, for Crosville were mounted on reconditioned Leyland Tiger TS7 chassis. Known as the Rivaloy body, the design was an improved version of that supplied to Argentina. Built in four sections and manufactured on jigs, they were completed ready for assembly onto the chassis.

The bodies were of a three bay construction, complete with a porch-type rear entrance. A one-piece entrance door was also hinged to open towards the front of the bus. The emergency door was fitted behind the cab and the body was finished to Tilling standards. The side panels were also extended, a replacement for the usual lifeguard rail. This gave the body a heavy appearance. On completion, the bus weighed 6 ton 4 cwt 2 qrs.

The first body was completed in November 1949, and in March the following year, the last of the 14 bodies was delivered to Crosville.

Fleet no.	Reg. no.	Vehicle	Bodywork
KA 1-10	FM 9965-9974	Leyland Tiger TS7	B35R
KA 12-15	FM 9976-9979	Leyland Tiger TS7	B35R

An offside view of the first Rivaloy single deck body supplied to Crosville on a Leyland Tiger chassis. It carried the fleet number KA1 and registration number FM 9978.

A rearward interior view of a Rivaloy single deck body supplied to Crosville. The Saunders' bookmaker transfer is visible on the right hand partition. Bodies for the Lincolnshire Road Car Company were finished in a similar Tilling style.

Commer Avenger demonstrators

The Anglesey factory produced two Commer Avenger demonstration vehicles which represented a further development of the Rivaloy body. They were the first bodies to carry the new design featuring a front dome and windscreen set in a full width front incorporating the Commer radiator grille assembly.

Using the Sao Paulo bodies as a basis, the new windscreen design was based on experiments carried out in the factory. The final design was heavily influenced by contemporary South American practice. Both featured a very rounded and deep front dome, including flat glass windscreens recessed into the window pan.

Each body was fitted with a front entrance containing double folding entrance doors. Opposite these, an emergency door was positioned behind the driver's seat. Externally, the lower panels behind the rear wheels curved upwards towards the rear of the body. These were the first two bodies fitted with the characteristic Saunders-style lifeguard rail. Situated at the bottom of the side panels, the rail was set-in at the front, towards the centre line of the front wheels.

Saunders completed one of the bodies as a demonstration vehicle. It had bus seating and sliding ventilators were fitted to the side windows. Decorative polished aluminium mouldings were attached to the waist rail and the completed vehicle had an unladen weight of 4 ton 18 cwt 2 qrs.

The second body was finished to a higher standard with coach seating. It had half drop, wind down windows of the RT pattern along the sides. Externally, it was given a two-colour paint scheme and featured distinctive square wings. The unladen weight of this vehicle was 5 ton 1 cwt 2 qrs. In 1950, Saunders exhibited this vehicle at the Commercial Motor Show and it was registered at the end of the same year.

Both vehicles were sold for non-PSV use. However, the coach version eventually became a PSV, used by Cullings of Claxton and later Mid Wales Motorways who were still the owners when the vehicle was destroyed by fire. LYL 169 eventually began work as a public service vehicle when it was sold to the firm of T W Mundy, based in Camborne, who traded as Silver Queen. This business later passed to Grenville, also of Camborne.

Fleet no.	Reg. no.	Vehicle	Bodywork
—	OUA 76	Commer Avenger	DP31F
—	LYL 169	Commer Avenger	B31F

One of two Rivaloy
bodies fitted to Commer
Avenger chassis. This bus
version was fitted with a
destination blind from a
Cuban body.

Looking forward inside
the coach body fitted
to a Commer chassis.
It had RT-style,
opening windows.

The coach type Rivaloy body fitted to the Commer Avenger chassis. The registration
number of this vehicle was OUA 76.

Some of the first Leyland Royal Tigers destined for Cuba are loaded aboard a ship at Hull docks. In all 620 made the long sea journey.

1950

Autobuses Modernos SA Cuba

Leyland Motors sub-contracted Saunders to build bodies for this important Cuban export order. At the time it was said to be worth approximately 10.5 million dollars and called for the supply of 620 Leyland Royal Tiger chassis fitted with Rivaloy dual doored, single deck bodies. Autobus Modernos was a new company formed under a

One of the first Rivaloy single deck bodies supplied to Cuba. The roof marker lights, the fleet number transfers and the Royal Tiger badge had yet to be fitted.

The interior of the Rivaloy body style supplied to Cuba. A Leyland Royal Tiger badge was fixed to the bulkhead over the windscreen.

franchise granted by the Cuban government. It replaced the antiquated Cuban tramway system and existed in its current state until such time as the operation became debt free. Once this objective was achieved, the company reverted back to state ownership under the Cuban government.

To fund the venture, the company planned to use the fares collected on the vehicles. Under the contractual agreement, the supplied buses would remain the property of Leyland Motors until the debt had been repaid. The contract was signed in June 1950 and included the general manager's request for the building of four additional buses to act as demonstration vehicles. The first of the four demonstrators was completed

A typical shipment of buses to Cuba at Hull docks. Each completed bus is accompanied by chassis loaded with PKD body parts for further vehicles.

in July 1950 and subjected to extensive testing at MIRA before work on the main contract could begin.

The order required the delivery of 327 completed buses of which 73 were completed but only finished externally in primer paint. The remaining bodies were supplied in partially knocked down (PKD) form. The company started delivering the buses in December 1950 and completed the order in September the following year. Apart from the construction of the four demonstration buses, chassis delivery from Leyland did not begin until July 1950 with the last one arriving at the factory in December of the same year. The late deliveries heavily influenced a decision in September 1951 to reduce the order for 620 buses to 568, excluding the four demonstration vehicles.

The first body completed in July 1950 was different to the main production ones. The opening window in the rear side bay was omitted and the lower rear panels were curved, rather than straight, at the bottom. This curved shape was similar to the bodies built on the Commer chassis. Some of the metal fabrication work was sub-contracted to another coachwork builder, Metalcraft of Blythe Bridge, Staffordshire. Although the exterior panels were fabricated from steel sheet, the roof, front and rear domes were all made from aluminium.

These single deck bodies were the first to be exported by the company in PKD form. Each delivery contained a number of completed buses and a number of PKD bodies mounted on their chassis.

The Rivaloy bodies were fitted with dual doors and early examples were delivered with flat glass windscreens. Vehicles in later deliveries were fitted with windscreens containing opening lower sections.

When completed, the bodies were finished in a white livery with a blue waistband and a front panel V pattern. Many of the buses were shipped through Hull docks.

One of the demonstration buses was displayed on the Leyland stand at the 1950 Commercial Motor Show. An interesting feature was that the components of the vehicle were visible through transparent panels in the saloon floor.

All the supplied bodies were mounted on LOPSU1/1, left hand drive chassis. Each bus provided seating for 40, with provision for 22 standing passengers.

All illustration showing the components of the Rivaloy single deck body supplied in PKD form to Cuba.

An interior view of the Rivaloy single deck body mounted on a Leyland Royal Tiger chassis for the Anglo Iranian Oil Company. The vehicles were fitted with unusual three and two wooden slat seating. This bus may have been one of the four Cuba demonstration vehicles altered to suit its new owner.

Anglo Iranian Oil Company

The Anglo-Iranian Oil Company ordered one dual-doored Rivaloy single deck body of the Cuban design. It was mounted on the first left hand drive Leyland Royal Tiger LOP SU1/1 chassis. Internally, it was fitted with wooden slatted 'three and two' seating. This arrangement provided an estimated seating capacity for 51 people.

Maidstone & District Motor Services

Following the development of the single deck Rivaloy body Saunders decided to produce a new double deck design, using the same principles of construction.

The first double deck Rivaloy body was mounted on a reconditioned Bristol K5G chassis. It formed part of an order for two Rivaloy bodies and included the production of a single deck body. The latter was designed to include a rear entrance covered by

Fleet no.	Reg. no.	Vehicle	Bodywork
S02	GKR 612	Bristol K5G	B35R
DH 11	GKR 741	Bristol K5G	H30/26R

The first Rivaloy double deck body mounted on a reconditioned Bristol K5G chassis for Maidstone & District.

a sliding door. The single deck body was mounted on a reconditioned Bristol L5G chassis and was registered as GKR 612, fleet number S02.

Saunders new double deck body was of four bay construction, strongly resembling the London Transport RT double deck style. The jigs used to produce the London design may well have been used in the manufacture of the Maidstone & District double deck body. The upper and lower deck windows were of a similar size and resulted in the use of deep lower deck side panels. Other London design features were copied including the use of a sliding door to the cab, the rear upper deck emergency door and the dished panels at the rear of the lower saloon windows.

The completed bus weighed 7 ton 7 cwt and was finished in the green and cream Maidstone & District livery.

Lincolnshire Road Car Co.

The Lincolnshire Road Car Company ordered a single Rivaloy body, supplied on a reconditioned AEC Regal chassis. Finished to the Tilling standard, the body was similar to those produced for Crosville, however, the lower body side panels were not as deep as those fitted to the earlier bodies. A Saunders-style lifeguard rail was positioned beneath these panels, lightening the external appearance of the body.

A near-side view of the Rivaloy body, supplied to Lincolnshire Road Car on an ex-Enterprise & Silver Dawn AEC Regal chassis. At the bottom of the lower side panels, the Saunders-style lifeguard rail is clearly visible.

Fleet no.	Reg. no.	Vehicle	Bodywork
902	ABE 960	AEC Regal	B35R

The Rivaloy single deck, dual-doored body supplied on a Leyland Royal Tiger chassis for use in Florida. The lower rear side panel has a straight edge.

1951

Miami Transit Company, Florida

Early in 1951 Saunders built a dual-doored single deck body on a left hand drive Leyland Royal Tiger chassis. Styled to the Cuba design, the completed bus was supplied to the Miami Transit Company and numbered 900. This vehicle was perhaps produced as an attempt to break into the American market.

Compania Uruguaya de Transportes Colectivos SA

This company ordered 25 bodies, mounted on left hand drive Leyland Royal Tiger chassis. The commission was placed shortly after the order for the Cuba buses and both shared a similar body design. The Leyland Royal Tiger chassis arrived at the factory throughout April and May.

There were minor differences in the bodies produced for Compania Uruguaya de Transportes Colectivos when compared to the Cuban order. For example, the

One of the Leyland Royal Tigers supplied to C.U.T.C.S.A. photographed at work in 1994. Apart from missing a side locker door, the body is very much as originally built. (Copyright M. Fenton)

An exterior view of one of the Rivaloy bodies supplied to C.U.T.C.S.A. complete with its three rails along the side windows and a straight bottom to the rear lower panels.

emergency door in the rear saloon window was hinged at the bottom and externally three horizontal rails were fitted across the saloon windows on each side. The lower portions of the front windscreens also opened outwards for ventilation purposes, a feature incorporated into the bodies later delivered to Cuba. In addition, heavy steel channel bumpers were fitted across the front and rear of the body. The dual-doored bodies seated 40 people with provision for 22 standing passengers.

A Daimler CVD6 chassis bodied for Kumasi Municipal Transport, Gold Coast.

Kumasi Municipal Transport, Gold Coast

Kumasi Municipal Transport, which operated on Africa's Gold Coast, ordered six Rivaloy single deck bodies fitted to long wheelbase, vertical front-engined Daimler CVD6 chassis. Originally the order may have called for 20 bodies but in the event, Saunders only completed six of them.

The Cuban-style body was modified to suit the front engined chassis. However, the use of a deep, rounded front dome and the recessed front windscreen arrangement was retained. The radiator was covered with a unique full front design and the entrance and exit were fitted with two-piece folding doors. Full depth sliding windows were also positioned on each side of the body and the lower portions of the front windscreen openings were designed to provide ventilation in the saloon. A heavy duty chrome bumper was fitted across the front of the buses, the first of which was completed in June 1951 and tested at MIRA before shipment overseas. This dual-doored body was capable of seating 40 passengers.

Looking forward along the interior of a Rivaloy body supplied to Kumasi on Daimler CVD 6 chassis. The bell cord was fitted in the centre of the roof and a full-length rail fixed to the roof for standing passengers.

Lincolnshire Road Car Co.

A repeat order was received from this company for the supply of two further Rivaloy single deck bodies. These were mounted on reconditioned and lengthened pre-war AEC Regal chassis. Each had an overall length of 30ft and was produced in a similar design to those supplied during the previous year. They were both finished to the Tilling group specification.

Fleet no.	Reg. no.	Vehicle	Bodywork
773-4	HBE 260-1	AEC Regal	B39R

Maidstone & District Motor Services

In January 1951, work started on an experimental, all-aluminium alloy, double deck bus mounted on an AEC Regent Mark 111 chassis. Built using the Rivaloy principles of construction, this body had a unique upper deck floor system. It was of a cross-braced type again in the quest to reduce overall body weight.

On completion, the bus was sent in an unpainted condition to be tilt tested at the Edge Lane works owned by Liverpool City Transport. In September 1951 it was also extensively tested at the MIRA test track near Nuneaton. Once these tests were completed the vehicle was painted in a green and cream livery. The unladen weight of this 56-seat double deck vehicle was 6 ton 15 cwt 3 qrs.

In November 1951, the bus was registered by the Maidstone & District Company and entered service with their fleet number DH 500. Following its service with Maidstone & District, the bus passed to CB Law of Prestwick before moving to Dodds of Troon, a member of the AA Motor Service group. By 1994 it had passed into preservation.

Looking forward along the lower saloon of the lightweight body fitted to the AEC Regent double deck chassis.

The experimental lightweight design double deck body mounted on an AEC Regent Mark III chassis, photographed at MIRA and later, registered as OKM 317. Stress measuring equipment can be seen fitted in both saloons.

Erne Bus Co. Enniskillen

Two Rivaloy single deck bodies were supplied to this operator as shells for completion in its own workshops. Mounted on Leyland Royal Tiger PSU1/9 7ft 6in wide chassis, these bodies were fitted with Cuban style front and rear domes.

A large luggage rack was fitted on the rear of the roof. This was accessed by a ladder located at the rear nearside of the vehicle. An emergency door was also fitted in the centre of the rear of the body and a single fog lamp located in the front panel below the windscreen, between the headlamps.

Finally, a Saunders-style lifeguard rail was positioned below the body side panels, while at floor level an aluminium alloy moulding strip was fixed along the sides.

Fleet no.	Reg. no.	Vehicle	Bodywork
203-4	IL 5605/5698	Leyland RT PSU 1/9	B44F

One of the Erne bus Leyland Royal Tigers in the company of a Leyland Comet fitted with a locally built body. It has a substantial roof-mounted luggage rack.

Londonderry & Lough Swilly Railway

The four bodies ordered by this operator were also supplied as shells for completion. On their arrival to the dockside, they were mounted on Leyland Royal Tiger 7ft 6in wide, PSU1/9 chassis.

The bodywork was similar to those supplied to the Erne Bus Co. Ltd order except that the design included the use of a central entrance, located just forward of the rear axle, on the nearside. Once again, a luggage rack was fitted on the roof at the rear of the body and included an access ladder. Internally, full height partitions were used to totally enclose the driver's cab. A door was also provided in the partition to allow entry into this from the saloon.

Externally, a side destination display was fitted into the roof panels adjacent to the entrance door. A rear registration panel was also fixed at waist rail level in the rear emergency door. Finally, Saunders-style lifeguard rails were set below the side panels and an aluminium alloy moulding fitted at floor level down each side.

Fleet no.	Reg. no.	Vehicle	Bodywork
71-74	IH 9539/9725/9840/9841	Leyland RT PSU1/9	B44C

One of the Rivaloy Leyland Royal Tiger vehicles supplied to Lough Swilly Railway.
The partition around the driver's cab is visible through the nearside windscreen.
The entrance door is just in front of the rear wheel.

Argentine Government

In July 1951, Leyland Motors placed an order for 100 bodies. The request was made in connection with an Argentinian government order for 600 complete buses and 150 chassis. As sub-contractors to Leyland, Saunders-Roe supplied the Cuba-style Rivaloy dual-doored bodies mounted on Leyland Royal Tiger, left hand drive chassis.

The exterior panels were manufactured in aluminium alloy and an emergency door was fitted at the rear of the body. The driver's cab was fitted with an electric fan and one seat was designated solely for the use of the conductor. Interestingly, the entrance and exit doors were air operated. Seating was provided for 40 people and provision made for 22 standing passengers. Each body was finished in aluminium with a blue waistband and a V design was painted on the front panel.

The first vehicles were delivered in October 1951. The remainder were completed by April 1952 at the same time that the company was finishing the last units of the Cuba contract.

Penrhyn Castle's gate house provides a background for this photograph of one of the Rivaloy bodied Royal Tigers supplied to the Argentinian government.

1952

Saro single deck prototype

In 1951 design work had already started on a new lightweight, single deck body. The design, incorporating unique features, was transformed into a full-sized mock up built by the factory's experimental department. However, when they were shown the design with its unique features many operators disliked it and in February 1952, work started on a new design for an all-aluminium alloy, single deck body.

The new design, known as the Saro body, was mounted on a prototype Leyland Tiger Cub chassis. To save weight, the window bays were shallow and measured 3ft 11ins in width. When the prototype was being built, some of the aluminium alloy sections including the crib rail were unavailable so were fabricated using steel instead. As a result, the saloon floor was raised each side of the gangway and the access panels fitted on either side of the body were shallower than those fitted to production bodies.

Problems were also experienced with the chassis cooling system. To solve this an aperture covered with mesh was cut into the lower front panel and below the front windscreens and two air intakes were provided for a Webasto saloon heater. The latter

The prototype Saro Leyland Tiger Cub. The radiator air intake was fitted in the front lower panel while the vehicle also sported an in-swept lifeguard rail together with a non-standard crib rail moulding.

was experimentally fitted to this body and the aperture failed to appear on the later production bodies.

The curved front and rear panels together with the front and rear domes were constructed from aluminium alloy. On some of the later production bodies, the lower front panels were split into three pieces manufactured using reinforced glass fibre. In addition, the angle of the windscreen was increased from 20 degrees in the prototype to 22 degrees off the vertical.

Externally, the headlamps were mounted in the front panels on aluminium castings. On the front and sides, the crib rail was covered by a folded aluminium strip containing three ribs and flat ends. Semaphore direction indicators were provided on each side of the body with a direction arrow panel fitted over the rear registration plate. The driver's signalling window also had the small opening windows fitted at the top of it to match the saloon sliding ventilators. This was later altered to conform to the style of production bodies whose opening windows were fitted at the bottom.

Following the vehicle's completion in April 1952, it was extensively tested at MIRA. At the same time, the bus was photographed showing the number P22 in the numeral box. In the same month, Leyland registered the vehicle and it became a demonstration and test vehicle for them.

Looking towards the driver's cab along the lowered gangway of the Saro body fitted to the prototype Leyland Tiger Cub chassis.

In August, the bus finally entered service with Ribble in its original condition. It was later returned to Saunders-Roe to be brought into line with current body production. The external polished aluminium rubbing strip was also replaced with another style of moulding fitted to the sides, front and rear of the body. In 1955, before the bus was sold to Llynfi Motor Services of Maesteg in South Wales, the moulding and front panels were replaced with production items.

As a demonstration bus, the vehicle was finished in an all-red livery. Small Leyland Diesel lettering were also fitted beneath the driver's cab window and adjacent to the entrance door. The livery was relieved with the use of an aluminium moulding containing a plastic insert. This was fitted below the saloon windows on each side of the body, the front windscreen and across the entrance doors.

Fleet no.	Reg. no.	Vehicle	Bodywork
203-4	OTC 738	Leyland Tiger Cub	B44F

Great Northern Railway of Ireland

In keeping with previous deliveries of Rivaloy single deck bodies to operators within the Irish Republic, four bodies supplied to Great Northern Railway were delivered as complete shells. Mounted on 7ft 6in wide Leyland Royal Tiger PSU1/9 chassis, the operator completed construction in their own workshops.

In contrast to those delivered to Erne Bus Co. Ltd and Londonderry & Lough Swilly Railway, a cab door was fitted into the side. This allowed the cab to be separated from the saloon. Again, a roof mounted luggage rack and access ladder were fitted at the rear, together with a centrally positioned emergency door.

The Saunders-style lifeguard rail was positioned below the body side panels. The aluminium moulding fitted along each side of the body at floor level was polished rather than painted. At the front of the bus, a steel channel bumper was fitted below the headlamps and the single fog lamp.

Following the delivery of the shells in July 1952, the buses were finished in the attractive blue and cream GNR livery.

One of the Rivaloy single deck bodies supplied to the Great Northern Railway. The driver's cab was fitted with a door and the vehicle had a roof-mounted luggage rack.

Fleet no.	Reg. no.	Vehicle	Bodywork
225-28	ZO 3762/4076/4401, IY 8390	Leyland RT PSU1/9	B44C

The Saro-bodied Leyland Tiger Cub for Ribble that featured prominently on the Saunders-Roe stand at the 1952 Earl's Court Commercial Motor Show.

Ribble Motor Services

The second prototype Saro single deck body was mounted on a Leyland Tiger Cub chassis and displayed at the 1952 Commercial Motor Show.

This was the first body to feature a flat saloon floor. A slight ramp ran down the gangway from the area over the front axle to the floor adjacent to the driver's cab. A Clayton heater was mounted under the floor and warm air was fed into the saloon through ducts along the body sides. An air intake for the engine was also fitted in a panel on the offside of the body.

In comparison, the side access panels were deeper than those in the original Saro single deck body. The window finishers and the side panels, a non standard feature, were covered in Rexine. The front panels below the windscreens comprised of three sections and the external side panel joints were overlapped. Polished aluminium alloy extrusion rubbing rails were also fitted across the front, side and rear panels. A route number display was mounted in the rear dome over the centrally-fitted emergency door and the rear registration plate was fixed in the lower rear panel with a single rear light. The bus was finished in the Ribble livery and became the first of 50 similar buses ordered by the company.

Fleet no.	Reg. no.	Vehicle	Bodywork
408	ERN 776	Leyland Tiger Cub	B44F

Birmingham City Transport

May 1952 saw a start made on a Saunders-Roe designed, lightweight, all-aluminium alloy double deck body. Mounted on a Guy Arab lightweight BCT chassis and powered by a Gardner 6LW engine, it was built to the exact requirements of Birmingham City Transport.

Originally, it may have been intended for use as a prototype for a contract to supply 100 similar bodies to the operator, but in the event, they were never built. However, this

The Saro double deck bus built to the design of Birmingham City Transport on a Guy Arab chassis. It carried the fleet number 3001 and registration number LOG 301.

vehicle became one of the three experimental lightweight double deck buses placed in service by the operator for evaluation purposes. Constructed in jigs from aluminium alloy sections, the completed body outline was unlike any other double deck body produced at Beaumaris. The vehicle had an unladen weight of 7 ton 4 cwt 2 qrs. For certification purposes, the bus was tilt tested at the Edge Lane Works of Liverpool City Transport. Afterwards, it was exhibited on the Saunders-Roe stand at the 1952 Commercial Motor Show. In 1953, the bus was fitted with a Gardner 5LW engine. This was retained throughout its service in the Birmingham fleet which started in the same year. Following its withdrawal, the bus was purchased for preservation.

Devon General Omnibus & Touring Co.

This company ordered a Rivaloy body that was the lightest of all the double deck bodies produced at Beaumaris. It was mounted on a reconditioned AEC Regent chassis rebuilt by Devon General using double deck frames and Regal running units.

The external appearance followed the RT outline and incorporated a number of features including dished panels behind the lower deck windows, the sliding cab door and the rear upper deck emergency door. The width of the window bay was the same as the Saro single deck body and many of the parts including the window pans and

Looking towards the rear of the upper deck of one of the bodies supplied to Devon General. It had RT-style window finishers and an emergency window at the rear.

A rear view of the lightweight double deck body supplied to Devon General.
The RT body features can be clearly seen. The step in the body side was to assist the
conductor to change the side destination blind.

Fleet no.	Reg. no.	Vehicle	Bodywork
DR 705	ETT 995	AEC Regent III	H30/26R

glazing were used. The body weighed 1 ton 19 cwt which was 5 cwt lighter than that
fitted to the AEC Regent Mark III chassis. The unladen weight of the completed bus
was 5 ton 19 cwt.

In February 1953, the vehicle left the factory with the registration number NUO 681.
Before entering service, the bus was given the registration ETT 995 from an AEC
Regal single deck bus as well as the fleet number DR705.

Devon General used the vehicle in trials alongside a Weymann bodied AEC Regent
Mark III double deck bus previously shown on the Weymann Stand at the 1952
Commercial Motor Show. The company used the trials to determine its future vehicle
purchasing policy. Eventually these trials turned in the favour of the lightweight
double deck bus. However, it was to remain the sole example of its type and was
later acquired by the West of England Transport Museum for preservation and
eventual restoration.

A completed Leyland Royal Tiger with its open side luggage locker ready for delivery to Auckland, New Zealand.

Auckland Transport Board

In 1952, a large order from New Zealand was placed with Saunders-Roe for Rivaloy single deck bodies. Production began on the first batch of them in March of that year and was completed by June. The bodies were then stored on stands awaiting delivery of the Leyland Royal Tiger chassis.

Produced for the Daimler Freeline, the order followed that for Rivaloy single deck bodies. The first Leyland and Daimler buses were completed in December 1952 and the first batch of vehicles shipped to New Zealand aboard the SS Pipiriki in January 1953. A number of BUT trolleybuses were also ordered around this time.

The Auckland order called for most of the bodies to be supplied in partially knocked down kits. This requirement was a crucial part of the previous Cuban contract. The floored chassis were sent from the factory in batches and carried sufficient parts for the construction of three bodies. However, 25 of the bodies for the Leyland Royal Tiger chassis were completed at Beaumaris, before shipment.

The bodies on the Leyland and Daimler chassis were 33ft long. The entrance and exit doors were operated either pneumatically or electro-hydraulically and a treadle mat was fitted in the centre exit steps to prevent the doors closing while a passenger was in the process of leaving the vehicle. The bodies fitted to the Daimler chassis differed from those on the Leyland version. They had a modified front dome to accommodate the higher driving position on the Daimler chassis.

The first Auckland Daimler Freeline at Beaumaris with the wrong fleet number.

Looking forward, an interior view of a Rivaloy body mounted on a Daimler Freeline chassis for Auckland.

The first Auckland Daimler Fleetline in service with the fleet number altered from 150 to 201 and the roof repainted.

Lorries collect BUT trolleybuses built for Auckland from Beaumaris on the first leg of their long journey to New Zealand.

The interior of one of the Auckland trolleybuses. Rails for standing passengers were fitted to the roof.

Three of the Auckland BUT trolleybuses in their grey primer stand at Beaumaris awaiting collection.

A further minor external difference was the shape of the sidelights in the front panel. The Daimler had circular ones while the Leyland sidelights were rectangular in shape.

The first Daimler vehicle completed at the factory was incorrectly numbered 150. Before entering service, the vehicle was given fleet number 201.

The Leyland chassis supplied against this contract were unusual in having AEC pre-selective gearboxes, to match the gearbox fitted to the Daimler. Similar bodies were also supplied for the Bedford SB chassis and these resembled those built on Daimler chassis to Kumasi the previous year. These were built in 1954 with delivery completed in 1955.

The BUT trolleybus chassis were fitted with the first and only Saunders-Roe trolleybus bodies. These were built to resemble the bodies supplied to Auckland by other manufacturers. In January 1954, the first BUT ETB1 chassis were delivered to Beaumaris and assembly completed in September of the same year. In 1957, the last completed vehicles entered service in New Zealand. The trolleybuses were 8ft 6in wide and 35ft long. The window bays were smaller than those used in the standard Rivaloy design.

The three trolleybus bodies were supplied in a grey primer paint finish. However, the factory-completed Leyland and Daimler units were finished in a livery of lettuce green, deep cream and silver with a lining in larch green.

All of them were fitted with a side destination display in the roof panel adjacent to the front entrance. A large open locker was provided in the lower panels between the axles for the storage of prams and pushchairs. Glass louvres were positioned over the opening side windows and steel channel bumpers were fitted to the front and rear of the body. Members of the Beaumaris Saunders-Roe staff travelled to New Zealand to supervise the erection of the PKD bodies in the Auckland workshops.

Fleet no.	Reg. no.	Vehicle	Bodywork
201-290	—	Daimler Freeline D650HS	B44D
451-500	—	Leyland Royal Tiger OPSU1/1	B44D
60-99	—	BUT ETB1	B45D
301-312	—	Bedford SB	B35D

1953

Londonderry & Lough Swilly Railway

This operator made a repeat order for four Rivaloy single deck bodies. These were supplied as shells for mounting on Leyland Royal Tiger PSU1/9 chassis by the company. Once again, the body shells were mounted on the chassis at the dockside. One of them was damaged while being loaded aboard ship at Holyhead. It was returned to Beaumaris for repair before being sent on its way again. These 7ft 6in wide buses were similar to those supplied two years earlier in 1951.

The Saunders-Roe Leyland Comet articulated delivery lorry carries a Lough Swilly body shell from Beaumaris on the first leg of its journey to Ireland.

Fleet no.	Reg. no.	Vehicle	Bodywork
75-78	UI 5135/5205/5325/5726	Leyland RT PSU1/9	B44C

The demonstration Saro Leyland Tiger Cub supplied to London Transport, photographed at the Chiswick Works.

Leyland Motors

In February 1953, construction started on the first production Saro single deck bus body. It was different to the previous prototypes as the depth of the side windows was increased by two and a half inches to improve vision from the saloon interior. The body, mounted on a Leyland Tiger Cub PSUC1/3 chassis, was also fitted with a pneumocyclic direct action gearbox. The bus was finished in Green Line colours.

Before entering service with London Transport in June 1953, Leyland Motors service department used the bus in a series of time trials. These experiments demonstrated the ease with which the main units could be removed from the chassis and replaced. London Transport also evaluated the bus as a possible replacement for the AEC Regal Mark IV single deck buses it had recently placed in service.

The bus was returned to Leyland after a year and in 1958 was presented to the company employees' social club.

Fleet no.	Reg. no.	Vehicle	Bodywork
—	PTE 592	Leyland Tiger Cub PSUC1/3	B44F

The Guy Arab LUF chassis bodied by Saro as a demonstration vehicle for Guy Motors, stands outside the gatehouse of Penrhyn Castle.

Guy Motors

This was the first and only Saro single deck body to be placed on a non-Leyland Tiger Cub chassis. Built on a lightweight Guy Arab LUF chassis, it was manufactured as a demonstration vehicle for Guy.

The completed bus was finished in a livery of red and cream. Its body featured a destination display and separate triple route number display. The Saro body was almost identical to those built on the Leyland chassis and illustrated the ease with which it could be fitted to alternative makes of chassis.

In September 1953, Northern General was the first operator to use the new vehicle. Afterwards, it became a demonstrator. In 1955, it was sold to Samuel Morgan of Armthorpe. Later, the vehicle was sold on again, this time for preservation.

Fleet no.	Reg. no.	Vehicle	Bodywork
—	LJW 336	Guy Arab LUF	B44F

Kumasi Municipal Transport, Gold Coast

In September 1953, Saunders completed the first of 17 Rivaloy bodies mounted on Daimler Freeline D650HS chassis. These dual-doored units were similar to those supplied under the Auckland contract. In each of the main window bays, they were fitted with full depth, sliding windows. The lower portion of the windscreen also opened. A ribbed, polished aluminium moulding strip was fitted along each side of the body and large chrome bumpers were also fitted to the front and rear.

Originally the order may have called for the supply of 20 bodies, but in the event, only 17 were supplied in late 1953 and early 1954. The buses were capable of carrying 44 seated passengers and 22 standing.

A single deck Daimler Freeline for Kumasi Municpal Transport.

Irish Army, Dublin

A one-off Rivaloy single deck body mounted on a 7ft 6in wide Leyland Royal Tiger PSU1/9 chassis was bought by the Irish Army. It was similar to those produced for Erne Bus in 1951 and was supplied as a shell for completion in the Irish Republic. This vehicle was still in existence, though in poor condition, in 1994.

Fleet no.	Reg. no.	Vehicle	Bodywork
—	ZU 5000	Leyland RT PSU1/9	B44

Maidstone & District Motor Services

Due to this operator's interest in lightweight buses, the Beaumaris design team explored the possibility of using the Saro design as a basis for building an even lighter single deck vehicle. At the time, the elimination of the chassis frame was thought to successfully reduce weight and thus produce the desired savings in fuel costs.

Before the project could start the team required knowledge of chassis design. Two engineers, Wallace Owen and Arthur Beebee, were recruited from Crossley Motors. In February 1953, work started on building the underframe and was finished just two months later. The new body was designed for fitting onto the underframe.

The Saro body comprised seven transverse bearers attached to the body crib rail. Five of these were I-sections constructed from aluminium alloy. Another bearer consisting of a U-section was used to carry the rear engine mounting and the gearbox. The other tubular member was fitted at the front of the vehicle. Over the front and rear axles, two longtitudinal members, formed from aluminium into U-sections, were used to carry the road spring brackets and shackles. Over the engine, two tubular beams were positioned between the transverse bearers. Finally, a single beam was placed immediately in front of the engine and behind the bearer, situated to the rear of the front axle. Gusset

The lightweight integral single deck bus is photographed at MIRA while undergoing testing on October 1, 1953.

plates, fixed to the top and bottom of the beam, were used to reinforce the single beam fitted to the centre of the underframe.

The resulting underframe was far from conventional in its design. In order to reduce running costs the team bought in running units in the form of a Gardner 5HLW engine,

Fleet no.	Reg. no.	Vehicle	Bodywork
S068	RKE 540	M&D Gardner 5HLW	B43F

The underframe of the integral single deck bus as prepared for road testing before the body was attached. The underframe was strengthened by lengths of wood placed between the main frame. A temporary structure was placed around the front of the underframe attached to the wings and the perimeter frame.

coupled to a David Brown five speed gearbox. The fifth gear was an overdrive. A Kirkstall front axle was used in front and the rear axle was an Eaton two-speed unit. In order to reduce maintenance, the front and rear springs were fitted with Metalastik rubber-bushed spring shackle pins. Triple servo vacuum brakes were also fitted and an aluminium alloy, welded fuel tank was used to reduce the weight.

When completed, the bus had an unladen weight of 5 ton 17 cwt 3 qrs. However, the vehicle was designed to the specification of Maidstone & District and therefore, any potential production vehicles could have achieved further savings in weight. Before delivery to the operator, the bus underwent extensive testing at MIRA.

The Saro body fitted to the underframe differed from other units. An emergency door was placed in the rear offside and different front windscreens were used to those fitted in the standard version. The side access panels, the lower skirt panels and the entrance steps were all shallower.

The vehicle entered service in late 1953 and only the centre of the roof section was painted cream. The body carried two further versions of the Maidstone & District livery before it was eventually withdrawn from service. It was subsequently sold to Berresford Motors Ltd of Cheddleton from whom it was later purchased for preservation.

Leyland Motors

Leyland approached Saunders-Roe to create and construct an all aluminium lightweight double deck body to be mounted on an experimental rear engined, double deck underframe. Construction work on the underframe was already underway during the latter part of 1952 and by September the following year construction of the body had begun.

To reduce costs, the company used as many standard Saro parts as possible to build this one-off. The staircase was rearward ascending, rising over the rear mounted Leyland 0.350 turbocharged engine and AEC pre-selective gearbox. Both the gearbox and the turbocharged engine were transverse mounted across the rear of the

underframe. The driver entered the cab through a door fitted in the lower saloon bulkhead.

Designed to provide maximum forward vision, the full front body was fitted with

The experimental Leyland Lowloader STF 90 stands at Beaumaris after completion.

Leyland Lowloader STF 90 undergoes a tilt test in the body shop at Leyland. On each side there are examples of Leyland bodies, a double deck bus on the left and lorry cabs to the right.

deep front windscreens, although their depth was restricted due to the positioning of the fuel tank filler in the front panel. The side panels between the axles carried a polished aluminium extrusion of the style used on the Saro body. However, because of the attachment of the body pillars to the underframe this didn't cover the body mounting crib rail.

The rear upper deck emergency door was of the RT pattern. However, the rain strip fitted over the door featured the Leyland body S-shape. In order to save bodyweight, the upper deck floor was constructed using corrugated aluminium sheet, similar to the material used in Leyland's under frame. At the rear of the bus, two vertically hinged doors provided access to the engine. The engine coolant system filler and glass covered registration number plate were fixed above the doors. At the front of the bus, the sidelights were positioned below the headlamps. Before it was delivered to Leyland, the body was finished in a green livery, relieved by a cream upper deck panel and roof.

Following tilt testing in the body shop at Leyland the vehicle was returned to Saunders-Roe for the staircase to be altered. As a result, one seat was lost in the upper saloon and the staircase became forward ascending. At the same time, the canopy over the engine was modified to allow the coolant filler to be placed into the top of the canopy. The handrails for the staircase were also modified to provide a continuous rail running from the upper saloon waist rail down to the outermost edge of the engine canopy on the platform. Finally, the rear upper deck emergency door was altered to incorporate a two-glass design.

Once the alterations were complete, the bus was repainted. The upper deck panels were painted green while cream was used for the lower and upper deck window surrounds and roof. The unladen weight of the vehicle was 6 ton 17 cwt 3 qrs.

Leyland registered the vehicle in April 1954. The bus became a demonstration-test vehicle and was tried by many operators throughout the country. In 1954, it was shown in the demonstration park of the Commercial Motor Show. The Saunders-Roe vehicle became the most widely known vehicle of the two experimental rear engined Lowloader chassis. With the arrival of the Atlantean prototype double deck buses, the two Lowloaders were sold to Lowland Motorways in Glasgow.

Leyland also placed an order for a Saro single deck body fitted to a Leyland Tiger Cub PSUC1/5 chassis. On its completion in January 1954, the 7ft 6in wide bus was delivered with single wheels on the rear axle.

After using it as a demonstrator the Ulster Transport Authority decided to buy the vehicle. Eventually it was withdrawn from service and its new owner, who bought it for preservation, restored it to original livery.

Fleet no.	Reg. no.	Vehicle	Bodywork
—	STF 90	Leyland Lowloader	FH38 (37)/24R
—	PZ 4874	Leyland Tiger Cup PSUC1/5	B44F

Stormont Castle, Belfast provides a background to the Leyland Tiger Cub supplied to the Ulster Transport Authority as a demonstrator by Leyland Motors Ltd. The vehicle had single rear wheels.

Ribble Motor Services

The British Electric Traction group of companies placed an order for the supply of Saro single deck bodies fitted to Leyland Tiger Cub chassis. The first vehicle was delivered to Ribble Motor Services.

The first 49 were completed in December 1953. These were similar to the Ribble show bus, but the production bodies were fitted with deeper saloon windows. In conjunction with an experiment carried out by certain BET Group companies some, if not all, of the chassis were fitted with single wheels on the rear axle. However, these experiments to reduce fuel consumption were abandoned when it was revealed that their road holding capacity was compromised in poor weather conditions. The potential fuel savings also failed to live up to expectations.

In March 1954, the last buses were supplied to Ribble. Two of them from the production run, FCK 844 and FCK 884 were later preserved and restored to their original livery.

Fleet no.	Reg. no.	Vehicle	Bodywork
409-457	FCK 841-889	Leyland Tiger Cub	B44F

One of the production batch of Saro bodied Leyland Tiger Cubs for Ribble outside Fryars. The vehicle was fitted with single rear wheels.

The interior of the single deck body supplied on a Leyland Tiger Cub chassis to Ribble. The window finishers, side and rear panels are covered in non-standard Rexine.

1954

Yorkshire Traction

In April and May 1954, 24 Saro single deck bodies were supplied to Yorkshire Traction on Leyland Tiger Cub chassis. Externally, they differed from the previous vehicles supplied for this order. The front dome was modified to accept two single line destination displays alongside a triple route number display fitted to the nearside of the front dome.

Some of the completed buses were finished in an attractive red livery with cream window surrounds and a painted panel above the side windows. Other buses, for use on longer distance routes, were finished in a cream with a red roof and trim. The seating capacity remained the same in all the vehicles.

Fleet no.	Reg. no.	Vehicle	Bodywork
1002-1025	GHE 2-25	Leyland Tiger Cub	B44F

One of the Saro bodied Leyland Tiger Cubs built for Yorkshire Traction stands alongside Beaumaris Castle in March 1954. Fitted with semi-coach style seats, the vehicle was finished in the dominant cream livery relieved by red.

East Midland Motor Services

Between March and June 1954, 25 single deck Saro bodies mounted on Leyland Tiger Cub chassis were delivered to East Midland Motor Service. These vehicles were finished in the operator's distinctive chocolate, cream and biscuit livery. A single line destination display was positioned in the front dome alongside a route number display fitted on the offside.

Fleet no.	Reg. no.	Vehicle	Bodywork
R321-345	ORR 321-345	Leyland Tiger Cub	B44F

Leyland Tiger Cub, registration number ORR 341, supplied to East Midland Motor Services, ready to be delivered to its new owner.

Northern General Transport

Between July and September 1954, 15 Saro single deck bodies, mounted on Leyland Tiger Cub chassis, were supplied to Northern General Transport Company. All were finished in a red and cream livery. Unlike previously supplied Saunders-Roe bodies, there was not lined-out in the paintwork.

Fleet no.	Reg. no.	Vehicle	Bodywork
1543-1557	DCN 843-857	Leyland Tiger Cub	B44F

A Saro-bodied Leyland Tiger Cub of Thomas Bros, Port Talbot, South Wales. The bus, registration number NNY 71, stands in front of Beulah Chapel, at its original site in Groes village, Margam. The chapel was later moved to make way for the M4.

Thomas Bros, Port Talbot

Between May and July 1954, this small South Wales steel town-centred BET Group operator received nine Saro single deck bodies mounted on Leyland Tiger Cub chassis. Some, if not all of the buses were delivered in grey primer finish.

The operator finished the bodies in an unusual livery of turquoise blue and cream. The front dome contained a destination indicator without a separate route number display.

Fleet no.	Reg. no.	Vehicle	Bodywork
—	NNY 63-71	Leyland Tiger Cub	B44F

Liverpool City Transport

In January 1950, the Liverpool Transport Committee agreed for outside contractors to complete 50 Weymann body shells, mounted on AEC Regent Mark III chassis. Saunders-Roe was granted the task of completing 20 of these. However, Liverpool City Council wanted to grant the maximum amount of work possible to Merseyside firms and the Saunders work was eventually given to a local company.

In November 1951, Liverpool City Transport considered the need for fleet replacements. Orders were placed with AEC for the supply of 100 AEC Regent Mark III chassis. Of these chassis 38 were supplied with completed Crossley double deck

The unpainted AEC Regent built for Liverpool City Transport stands outside the works entrance on October 6, 1954.

bodies. Another 60 chassis were produced with Crossley double deck frames for completion by Liverpool City Transport. The remaining two bodies were supplied with Saunders-Roe lightweight aluminium, double deck bodies.

The two Saunders-Roe bodies featured a flat, square front and were designed to resemble the Crossley product, but the rear retained the upright profile of the RT design and the London style rear upper deck emergency door. Not surprisingly, maximum use was made of Saro body parts including window pans and glazing. A sliding cab door was also provided although London features including the dished panels behind the lower saloon windows were omitted. The completed vehicles had an unladen weight of 7 ton 6 cwt 2 qrs

One vehicle, fleet number A40, was supplied in an unpainted aluminium finish. It was the first unpainted bus to operate in the Liverpool fleet.

Both completed vehicles entered service in September and November 1954 respectively. These were the last double deck bodies produced by Saunders-Roe. Fleet number A40 was purchased for preservation and later formed part of the Mersey & Calder Bus Preservation Group.

The painted AEC Regent destined for Liverpool City Transport, fleet number A39 stands alongside Commer Superpoise Army truck chassis at Beaumaris.

Fleet no.	Reg. no.	Vehicle	Bodywork
A39-40	NKD 539-540	AEC Regent III	H32/26R

Leyland Motors

Completed in November 1954, a Saro single deck body was mounted on to a Leyland Tiger Cub chassis. Used as a demonstration vehicle for Leyland, the vehicle seated 38 passengers. This was the only Saro body to be fitted with a separate entrance and exit.

On each side of the body, deep sliding windows were fitted in three window bays and pram hooks were

An interior view of the Saro bodied Leyland Tiger Cub supplied as a demonstrator to New Zealand. The rear entrance door can be seen in the open position.

placed beneath the front windscreens. Internally, there were no luggage racks fitted. The vehicle was shipped to New Zealand and fulfilled its role as a demonstration bus. Afterwards, H & H Motors of Invercargill bought it and removed the rear exit. As a result, the seating capacity of the bus was increased to 40. It was still in service in 1994 and became the subject of a preservation project in New Zealand.

Trent Motor Traction

In July 1954, 10 Saro single deck bodies mounted on Leyland Tiger chassis were supplied to Trent Motor Traction. The operator received eight of these vehicles in grey primer finish. The remaining two were finished in red and cream. At the factory, a red panel was painted incorrectly above the side windows.

Fleet no.	Reg. no.	Vehicle	Bodywork
810-819	FCH 10-19	Leyland Tiger Cub	B44F

One of the two Saro-bodied Leyland Tiger Cubs painted at Beaumaris for Trent Motor Traction. Registration number FCH 19 has an incorrectly painted red roof stripe.

Four of the Saro-bodied Leyland Tiger Cub vehicles supplied to Sunderland and District Omnibus Company complete with their distinctive rear destination blinds.

Sunderland District Omnibus Co.

In August 1954, 16 Saro single deck bodies mounted on Leyland Tiger Cub chassis were delivered to this operator. The vehicles were finished in the blue and white livery of this Northern General subsidiary company. These bodies were different from previous orders. A destination display was centrally positioned in the rear dome, over the emergency door while deeper sliding ventilator units were fitted in three window bays on both sides of the body.

Fleet no.	Reg. no.	Vehicle	Bodywork
258-273	OUP 655-670	Leyland Tiger Cub	B44F

1956

Auckland Transport Board
New Zealand

In 1956, Auckland Transport Board placed a repeat order for 70 Rivaloy single deck bodies mounted on Daimler Freeline DH650HS chassis. In September that year, the first one was finished in a grey primer livery. Built to the same previous specification, the remainder were sent out to New Zealand in PKD units mounted on the chassis. Following completion in the operator's workshops, the buses entered service between 1956 and 1958. These were the last bodies produced by the company before Saunders-Roe was sold to the Hawker-Siddeley group in 1959.

An MCW-designed double deck body mounted on a Leyland Titan PD3 chassis for Brighton Corporation Transport. Fleet number 34 was registered as MCD 134F.

1968

Brighton Corporation Transport

In 1968, Laird (Anglesey) Ltd manufactured two batches of bodies in the Beaumaris factory. The production was carried out on behalf of MCW of Birmingham, a fellow member of the Laird group of companies. These were supplied to Brighton Corporation and Devon General.

The company produced five double deck bodies to the MCW Orion design. These were built on Leyland Titan PD3/4 chassis and parts were taken from Weymann's Addlestone factory. Work on the forward entrance, double deck vehicles began in March 1968. The buses were delivered to Brighton during June and July that year.

Fleet no.	Reg. no.	Vehicle	Bodywork
31-35 LUF	131-133F, MCD 134-135F	Leyland Titan PD3/4	H39/30F

Devon General Omnibus & Touring Co.

Built to the requirements of the operator, 10 MCW designed bodies were mounted onto Leyland Atlantean PDR1/1 rear engined double deck chassis. These were the first rear engined, double deck chassis to be bodied at Beaumaris since the experimental chassis of 1953. Sadly, they were also the last double deck bodies to be built there.

Production started in May 1968 with the first completed buses being delivered in October of the same year. The last vehicle delivered entered service in February 1969. One of these buses, fleet number 537, was purchased for preservation and repainted in its original livery.

Two of the Devon General Leyland Atlanteans shortly before delivery.

Fleet no.	Reg. no.	Vehicle	Bodywork
532-541	NDV 532-541G	Leyland Atlantean PDR1/1	H44/31F

Superior Coach Company of America

In the late 1960s the Superior Coach Company of America granted a licence to the MCW organisation to construct Superior body kits in the UK. The first was assembled at the Birmingham factory and the result was shown to the staff at Beaumaris. Following this, in June 1968, the Beaumaris staff assembled a similar body mounted on a Bedford VAM chassis. The vehicle was displayed in the demonstration park of the 1968 Commercial Motor Show.

Afterwards, the company received an order for 10 bodies assembled on left hand drive Bedford VAM chassis. These were sent to the Middle East for use by an oil company. Finally, a single body was also assembled on a Ford D-series chassis. This vehicle featured an entrance behind the front axle.

These were the last passenger carrying bodies produced at Beaumaris. It was the end of an important era in the bus building world.

A Superior body fitted to a Ford D-series truck chassis with Fryars in the background.

Production summary

1946 to 1956

Single deck bodies

Home market			Export market		
No.	**Chassis**	**Operator**	**No.**	**Chassis**	**Country/Operator**
18	AEC I	Northern General	60	Guy	Holland
24	Foden	Various	60	AEC	Lisbon
15	Guy	Various	50	AEC/ACLO	Argentine
25	Leyland	Midland General	91	AEC/ACLO	Brazil
1	Leyland	Northern General	572	Leyland	Cuba
14	Leyland	Crosville	1	Leyland	Iran
2	Commer	Demonstrators	1	Leyland	Miami
3	AEC	Lincs Road Car	25	Leyland	Uraguay
2	Leyland	Erne Bus	6	Daimler	Kumasi
4	Leyland	Lough Swilly	100	Leyland	Argentine
1	Leyland	Irish Army	90	Daimler	New Zealand
1	Leyland	Demonstrator	50	Leyland	New Zealand
4	Leyland	Lough Swilly	40	BUT	New Zealand
4	Leyland	Great Northern	12	Bedford	New Zealand
1	Leyland	Ribble	17	Daimler	Kumasi
1	SARO	Integral	1	Leyland	New Zealand
1	Leyland	Demonstrator	70	Daimler	New Zealand
1	Guy	Demonstrator			
1	Leyland	Demonstrator			
49	Leyland	Ribble			
24	Leyland	Yorkshire Traction			
25	Leyland	East Midland			
9	Leyland	Thomas Bros			
10	Leyland	Trent Motor Traction			
15	Leyland	Northern General			
16	Leyland	Sunderland District			
17	Bristol	Maidstone & District			

Export market Total = 1246

Home market Total = 272

Double deck bodies

Home market

No.	Chassis	Operator
9	Leyland	Southdown
40	Bristol	Maidstone & District
300	AEC	London Transport
1	Bristol	Maidstone & District
1	AEC	Demonstrator
1	Guy	Birmingham
1	AEC	Devon General
1	Leyland	Demonstrator
2	AEC	Liverpool

Total = 356

Export market

No.	Chassis	Country/Operator
20	AEC	Durban

Total = 20

Total number of bodies
Single deck 1,518
Double deck 376
Total 1,894

**Gerald Truran
1936–2005**